Sea-Side City

The Tides of Change Compilation

S.A. BALLANTYNE

Copyright © 2021 S.A. BALLANTYNE

All rights reserved.
The moral rights of the author have been asserted.

The characters and events in this book are fictitious. Any similarity to persons real, living or dead is coincidental and not intended by the author.

No part of this book may be reproduced, or stored in a retrieval system, or transmitted in any form or by any means, electronic, mechanical, photocopying, recording, or otherwise without express written permission by the author.

Cover Design: S.A. BALLANTYNE

Full Photo Credits by each cover page

NDP Logo & Sea-Side City Logo
created by S.A. BALLANTYNE

Copyright © 2019, 2020, 2021 S.A. BALLANTYNE

All rights reserved.

ISBN:
ISBN-13:

DEDICATION

To My Nanna
Isobel "Kay" Birch
1927 - 2010

The further back you stand the more that you will see,
don't just take it from me: go ahead and see.
An injection of rejection will ruin your perception, but the
projection of reflection will be closer to perfection and
the wonders that you ponder could help you live longer.

- S.A. Ballantyne

CONTENTS

Acknowledgments	I
Letter from an Anonymous Local	10
Map of Rockshore	11
Political Liabilities	13
Night Coat Origins	55
Untold Legend	97
Circle of Life	135
Surveying the Territory	173
The Fragile Mask of Porcelain	211
About Night Desk Publications (NDP)	250
Rockshore Messenger Articles	252
Sea-Side City – The Tides of Change Timeline	255

ACKNOWLEDGMENTS

Firstly I'd like to thank my mother (Lorraine) and my girlfriend (Charlette). Both of you have been incredibly supportive and loving: especially throughout this (self-inflicted) hectic time in my life.

Special thanks to David S Carlin
& my many other amazing friends
The Costers (Ty, Boris, Chrissy, Tilly and Rosie)
Danny, Ollie, Ant, Jack, Martin, Craig, Clarissa, Tom, Grace, Josie, Gemma, Hetti, Josh Ellis, Jason Miller, Lozz, Lloyd, James.

Additionally I'd like to thank a number of people who have motivated, inspired and assisted me at the right points in life:
Pete Bolton, Steve Tansey, Graham Brooks, Lindsey Smith, Mike Lever, Peter Palmer, Andy Simmonz, Nathan Mackenzie, Jon Patterson, Pat Davis, Jamie Howard, Mary Lenton, Keith Coleman & The Google Garage Team: Glenn White, Amy Stringfellow, Tom Myfield, Kirstie Kavanagh, Natalie & Daryl .

I would also like to thank you for taking the time to read

SEA-SIDE CITY

**The
Tides of Change
Compilation**

All characters, locations, articles, businesses, maps and adverts in this book and on sea-sidecityndp.com are a work of fiction which I have personally created.
Any similarities to people, locations, businesses or occurrences are purely coincidental.

- S.A. Ballantyne

Hello Stranger...

Whoever you are, I hope this finds you safe and well... Whether you are new to the city or a returning visitor, I advise caution.

Recently, someone I have known for years has died under suspicious circumstances. The police and the press have stated it is an ongoing investigation. But, I believe there is a killer on the loose! I have considered breaching the topic at the latest "Talk of the Town" meeting; an event where people from the community of Rockshore can gather to discuss local issues.

Sadly, the rest of the city seems more concerned with rumours of criminal enterprises in the derelict confines of South Town Harbour, all because of an article in the Rockshore Messenger. Drawing attention to myself is too much of a risk, besides, there might not even be a killer...

I guess everyone has their own lives to lead in Rockshore. There are people looking for work, friends and fulfilment. The question is: what are you looking for?

Take Care
- An Anonymous Local

CITY OF ROCKSHORE

KINGS-PORT HARBOUR

CARNINGSDALE

OUTSKIRTS

The Messenger Printing Office

Stockbridge Finances

St. Catherine's Hospital

NORTH SIDE

Rockshore Train Station

Lou's News

St. Catherine's Church

Community Centre

CITY CENTRE

Coastal-Collage Shopping Centre

The Job Centre

University Library

Penelope Park

Town Square

Town Hall

Cabot's Court Flats

"Cone-ee-Island" Ice Cream Parlour

Town Cryer Pub (The TC)

"Jacksville" Winstone-Way Council Estate

Audrey's Tea-Rooms

Parson's Care Home

"The Port in a Storm" Pub

Old Club House

Raven's-Dale Road (Pubs and Clubs)

Shopping Precinct (Cutting Craft Location)

INDUSTRIAL AREA

South Town Harbour (Condemned)

Student Halls of Residence

SOUTH SIDE

Family Funfair

High End Sea-View Housing

Seafront

Ferryport

Welcome to the Sea-Side City

COCKLESHORE ISLE (Neighbouring Island)

S.A. BALLANTYNE

Sea-Side City

Political Liabilities

Political Liabilities

Cover photo sourced from:
Pixabay

Uploaded by:
nextvoyage

POLITICAL LIABILITIES

It was a pleasant spring day in the latter weeks of May. The warm sun collaborated with a cool breeze to create the perfect day; however, ominous grey clouds lurked in the distance, signifying how quickly things could change. In contrast to the unpredictability of the weather, things rarely changed on the notorious Winston Way Council Estate, known to the locals of Rockshore as Jacksville. The Winston Way Council Estate had earned its moniker due to many of its balconies being draped with the Union Jack and the flag of St George. The area was notorious, known for being home to racists, criminals and jobless people. It had gained this reputation through numerous episodes of crime and antisocial behaviour in the area and the stigma associated with the flags. Indifferent to their undesirable reputation, two residents were making the most of the pleasant weather. Relaxing on their balcony, they discussed the prospects of an upcoming football match while enjoying cans of cheap booze. All was well in the world, until one of them noticed a hooded youth across the road trying to steal a bike.

"Oi, get your hands off that bike you thieving prick!"

they shouted, while hurling an empty can at the bike thief.

The carefree youth stuck his fingers up at them before taking off with his loot. Catching a glimpse of the situation unfolding from further down the street, Ginger Taylor thought to herself "Welcome to Jacksville" as she walked through the socially deprived urban wasteland. Ginger was making her way home from work at the council offices. To her relief, the two brutish lager louts went back into their flat. She continued down the street, greeted by crisp packets and various other forms of litter floating in the mild breeze. Eventually she encountered the bike thief, who insulted her short hair and conservative appearance as he made his getaway. Although she had become mildly resentful about how her life had turned out, her surroundings made her appreciate how it could be worse. She had a reasonably well-paid job and a rented flat, but somehow she felt something was missing.

She had dreamed of being a pop star when she was younger, then she aspired to be a soldier, and finally she wanted to be a political correspondent for the media. Gradually, her ambitions had become increasingly more realistic and increasingly less desirable. During her adolescence, her favourite popstar committed suicide after suffering a very public breakdown. As she matured, the horrors of war documented on the news steered her away from a life in the army. By the time she had decided to aspire to being a political correspondent, though her grades were adequate, Ginger had had enough of the educational system, so she decided to look for gainful employment. Eventually, her job hunt led her to an administrative role at the council offices. It had occurred to her that most of her ambitions in life were encouraged and discouraged by television reports. While distracted by her runaway train of thought, Ginger had left Jacksville and was subconsciously embarking on a detour towards the seafront. She slowly came back to reality as she noticed her reflection in a tinted window. Observing her slender physique, vibrant ginger bob haircut and subtly tanned complexion, she stared deeply until she could see her hazel eyes staring back at her. She came to question what she could do to make her life better. Shaking off her wandering thoughts, Ginger made her way back home. To avoid experiencing any more potentially depressing thoughts, Ginger put her earphones in and proceeded to listen to her selection of British Indy-rock music for the remainder of her journey home. Arriving at her humble rented flat in an area slightly classier than Jacksville, she chucked her keys down and threw herself back onto the bed, taking a moment to just lie there and stare at the ceiling. After a ready meal, several cups of decaffeinated tea and a few flying hours of substandard televised entertainment, it was time for her to go to sleep as she had bills to pay and work to attend the following day. The morning came as quickly as the night passed and Ginger was awoken by her half broken alarm clock ringing in her ear.

Rousing herself from her bed, she started to pick out her clothes for the day. All of a sudden she felt a sharp pain in her lower stomach. Unfortunately, this was the feeling of a dodgy ready meal. Following a sprint to the bathroom which could rival an Olympic runner's, she contacted her boss to inform him she would not be present for the day. Slightly peeved at the inconvenience of her sickness, he told her to come in if she felt better later.

One thing Ginger didn't like was being mistreated when she was ill. Despite being in a foul mood, she had the day off; Ginger hadn't spent a weekday in her dressing gown since she could remember. Taking some over the counter (potentially out of date) medication, she manually turned on her skip-scavenged 1980's television set. Being an incredibly frugal young lady, she often scavenged other people's unwanted goods.

Proceeding to starve out her ailment, Ginger lay back on her sofa nursing a sore stomach. After a few hours of being subjected to day time television, she realised she'd actually prefer to be at work, sore stomach or not. At roughly 12:30 her stomach seemed to have settled and she'd reached her wits end with the TV. After preparing a large bottle of water to see her through the day, Ginger got changed into her office clothes, releasing herself from the tediously banal programs she had suffered.

As a compromise, she decided she'd take a slow walk to buy her a bit more time. The warm weather eased her gently back into the outside world. On her approach to town, she saw an advertisement for the city's annual Talk of the Town.

The Talk of the Town event served as an open forum in which the residents of Rockshore could discuss various local issues. However, on further observation, she noticed that the event was being presented in association with Rockshore University. The event would take place in the Town Hall at 1 o'clock, which would be in ten minutes' time.

Realising that she hadn't taken much time to engage with current events in the city and still feeling perturbed by her boss's cavalier attitude; Ginger decided to attend. Nervously scanning her surroundings for colleagues who might have recognised her, she crept into the building.

Once she entered the refreshingly air-conditioned hall, Ginger was pleasantly surprised to see that the event had attracted a sizable turnout. The large crowd of spectators would make it easier for the rebellious young lady to remain undetected in her absence from work. Taking her seat in the corner of the room, Ginger started to settle in, anonymously observing the various people in attendance. Suddenly, she realised that the event had attracted camera crews from local news channels. Horrified at the potential risk of exposure, she wondered why the event had attracted coverage. Slumping anxiously in her chair she watched the other characters in the Town Hall.

She contemplated leaving, but before she was able to rise from her seat, she detected movement on the stage. A smartly dressed, balding man in a suit appeared on stage. As the audience became more aware of his presence, the chattering voices began to quieten.

Aware of the lowering levels of noise, the man's cheeks glowed as he stood smiling. Once he was satisfied he had the audience's attention, he began to address everyone.

"Good afternoon, ladies and gentlemen. My name is Neil Peterson; I am the coordinating lecturer for the Politics course at the University of Rockshore. As you may have already noticed, today's format for Talk of the Town will be somewhat different to what you might be accustomed to. Today's event will be hosted by our students, presenting us with an opportunity to engage with the city's issues together for the first time ever. You'll also notice that there are camera crews here. After pulling some strings, this historic event will be covered by our regional news channel.

This is because we wanted to showcase our bright young students and give them a chance to share their academic insights. Furthermore, it will give potential students across the country an insight into what they can achieve through studying at our fine university. Now I shan't go on for too much longer, but I'd just like to say there will be an opportunity for you to get involved in the debate later, if you're feeling brave enough."

After the chuckles had died down, the students entered and took their seats at the long table which had been set up on the stage. Some of them seemed nervous and others confident. One of the young men, dressed in a checked shirt and purple skinny jeans, kept sweeping his hair off his face as he fought through his nerves to explain the proceedings.

"Ok, so I know there's a lot to get through today, but first I'd like to offer some guidelines for this event. I feel that it is important to not discriminate against people's gender, race, creed or colour. So therefore, when I address members of the audience, I will describe the clothing you are wearing. We as a collective group have decided this is the best way to make the audience feel comfortable. This way you are not limited to the labels of your gender."

As the young man continued to pontificate, Ginger looked around the room. She noticed how bemused the members of the public looked. Ginger felt it was important for people's social identities to be respected.

However, she also started to question how it was relevant to addressing the city's issues. Although she hadn't attended the event in several years, Ginger had never experienced or heard of any incidents of discrimination at a Talk of the Town event.

A rather irritated looking girl seated at the end of the student panel pushed her glasses up her nose. She had straight brown hair, a black and white striped jumper and a sour face which looked used to sulking. Just before her colleague had finished speaking, she too started to address the audience:

"My name is Michelle Corrigan and I am a course rep for politics studies and president of the Feminist Rights Society. This is an issue which I would like us all to address, even though I only have knowledge of it happening at the university at this time.

I have been utterly shocked and disgusted to see that some of our male students have been looking at 'lad's mags' in the university café. I know some of you are not aware of this, but these magazines are degrading and offensive to women. They portray them as sex objects and can often contribute to cases of rape. I would like to put forward a motion that these magazines be banned throughout the university campus. Furthermore, I would like to encourage the audience to stop supporting these magazines. This filth represents the low-behaviour and savage nature often expressed in today's society. Together we can start to rebuild this country's dignity and stop the tyranny."

The majority of the students in the audience started to cheer and applaud, while the rest of the audience looked confused and quietly perturbed by the arguably misplaced anger the passionate young lady was displaying. There was an underlying sense of unrest within the audience.

They had attended the event to learn about and resolve issues regarding the city. Usually the presenter of the event would have invited them to participate by now.

All of a sudden a disgruntled man shouted out:

"Are we going to get a chance to talk or what? We want to know about what's going on with South Town Harbour, not your bloody uni!"

Much to the chagrin of Mr Peterson and the students, the man's outburst generated a rally of support from other members of the community in attendance. Michelle's face became flushed with rage. Seeing a combustible situation in the making, Neil Peterson returned to the stage and interjected:

"Ah yes, well thank you Michelle. While there is definitely merit to what you and Simon were saying, maybe we should turn our attention to more domestic issues around the city."

After finessing the altercation, Mr Peterson invited one of the other students to speak because of their local knowledge:

"Allister Benedict, have you got anything you want to add to this presentation?"

The young man's beady eyes darted around the room in contempt. Hunching over he spoke into the microphone with a passive aggressive tone:

"Well, if people can contain themselves for a moment.

Now, derelict building sites sealed off to the public don't worry me that much. I suggest that we worry less about modern urban myths like South Town Harbour and more about safe havens for racism and nationalism like the Winston-Way Estate, aka Jacksville.

The Rockshore Messenger isn't a reliable source of information; if you want to get to the true issues you have to read deeper.

How you can be more concerned about an opinion poll regarding a condemned harbour than an estate which flies the Union Jack like it's the 60's is beyond me!

We want to discuss the more relevant issues that affect us all. If you listen to us, you might gain more of an insight into what you can do to make positive changes for the better.

People have been deluded by fictional stories, misled by

facts for too long.

Take religion, Christianity for instance. The further people move away from the Bible the better people become. Maybe if we knocked down the churches around Rockshore and dedicated facilities to educating the flag-waving residents of Jacksville to see the error of their bigoted ways, there wouldn't be a need for meetings like this!"

A number of the students congregated around the front row erupted with applause at the revolutionary idea their peer had just proposed. Neil Peterson felt a sense of encouragement from his students' roar of support. Visibly delighted, his lips pressed together as he tried to contain his excitement.

Unbeknown to Mr Peterson or his students, Allister's comments had enraged several members of the audience. As the tension mounted, suddenly an angry middle-aged man rose from his seat in the audience and bellowed:

"You're not taking my church away, you heathen, tax-dodging piece of sh…"

The man's enraged roar snapped Neil Peterson out of his feel-good moment. The dumbfounded lecturer frantically waved his arm, signalling for the event staff to encourage the man to leave before he could finish his sentence.

With enraged vigour, Allister smugly exclaimed

"Thank you for proving my point you uneducated, illiterate delinquent. This is exactly what I'm talking about!"

As the infuriated man was escorted out, Allister added

"Maybe the lesser read members of the audience should leave the talking to us and try to learn something."

Some members of the audience were seething in anger; others were terrified of being intellectually embarrassed.

The other members of the student panel attempted to break the awkward silence and regain popularity and humour by each adding "I second that."

Ginger wondered why she was still there, at this point. The prospect of being informed of what was occurring in the city and hearing other people's points of view had dwindled. All of a sudden, her train of thought was interrupted as a young man with shoulder length blonde hair, sporting a scruffy looking beige parka jacket and jeans emerged from the shadows of the corner of the room.

He'd been sitting directly in front of Ginger; now he made his way down to the stage.

Catching Neil off guard, he took the microphone from his hand. Neil's face filled with shock as he recognised the young man. Once again, Mr Peterson waved for security; however, this time they didn't come.

Tapping the microphone to check it was still working, the mysterious gate-crasher stuck his thumbs up at the security guards, signalling he'd take two minutes; then he began his speech with a distinctive but unidentifiable accent:

"Okay, let's have a proper gander at this ill-thought propaganda.

This event is about issues around the city and by the looks of things, one has certainly been made apparent.

There's quite a large set of buildings in the city owned by the University of Rockshore. Now, universities are supposed to enhance people's knowledge and provide them with an array of social opportunities.

Today we've learned that not only could these idiots fail to comprehend the concept of this task, but they have demonstrated a total lack of social understanding.

I suppose it hasn't been a total waste of time though. Talk of the Town 2012 has proved that Rockshore University is about as valuable to the city as the derelict docks of South Town Harbour."

Ginger scoffed in amused disbelief; the local members of the audience erupted with cheers, laughter and applause at the young man's refreshing perspective.

Red-faced and outraged, Neil Peterson's eyes widened with embarrassment. The panel of students started to confer among themselves in disbelief at the audience's response.

Once the laughter had quietened, Michelle took the opportunity to respond

"That's all well and good coming from a failed undergraduate drop out like you Andrews.

Who do you think you are?"

A half grin spread across the mysterious young man's face

Momentarily tuning out from the ongoing debate, Ginger noticed that Neil Peterson was at the side of the stage, nervously holding his mobile. Unaware he was being watched due to the spectacle unfolding onstage, Mr Peterson reluctantly answered the call.

Upon answering the call, Ginger noticed a look of shock glaze over Mr Peterson's face. As he ended the phone call, he seemed to be rendered incapable of moving.

A roar of laughter from the crowd drew Ginger's attention back to the ongoing verbal exchange.

"The sad thing is, I happened to know several students from Rockshore Uni who could have worked with the city to try and resolve these issues. But instead, Peterson picks these sanctimonious sycophants to look down on everybody and regurgitate what passes as their useless assignments."

Following the young man's comments, Neil Peterson managed to pull himself out of his dumbfounded state and storm the stage once more.

"Okay ladies and gentleman I think it's time to bring this to a close. Unfortunately, Mr Andrews here has ruined it for everyone."

With that, Neil Peterson and his students started to leave, visibly enraged by the outcome of the event.

Following their exit, the young man addressed the

audience once more:

"Ah bollocks to that, why don't we stay here and have a proper Talk of the Town meeting?

Name's Jack by the way."

Though she was astounded and somewhat entertained by Jack's charismatic hijacking of the event, Ginger realised that the news cameras were still rolling and capturing the audience. In a moment of panic, she realised the time, and that she still wanted to go to work. She got up and sneaked out.

Jack noticed her leaving; however, he respected her wishes to leave and didn't draw any attention to her.

Jogging down the road she wondered if any of her colleagues would see her on the news that night. All the stress of worrying about it started to aggravate her stomach again. In a swift change of heart, she ran back home down the side streets to avoid detection.

Once she arrived ,she was obliged to visit the toilet once again. Though in discomfort, Ginger always appreciated the thinking environment the toilet presented.

She pondered the events of the day. Looking at her cold tiled bathroom floor, her imagination pursued answers as to what kind of a life Jack must have led to enable him to commandeer such an intimidating environment with such ease. Furthermore, she questioned what would motivate him to do such a thing.

A short while later, back at the town hall, the Talk of the Town event came to a close.

Following the departure of Neil Peterson and his students, the audience had relaxed and engaged in a more satisfying discussion.

After the event had come to a close, Jack made his way off the stage, with his sights set on the pub. Before he could make it past the crowd, he found himself accosted by a local journalist.

The journalist grabbed his hand, pumping it up and

down as he introduced himself:

"Hector Diamond, Rockshore Messenger. You may have read my article on South Town Harbour."

Unable to escape the sweaty grasp of Hector's hand, or the heaving crowd blocking the exit, Jack found himself being pressured into a post-event interview. Having generated interest in his recent article, Hector was hungry to maintain his momentum as an up and coming journalist.

Furthermore, fate had presented him with the perfect opportunity to interview the young upstart who had hijacked a televised event. Relishing the moment, Hector launched in by questioning Jack about the visible animosity between himself and his former lecturer.

Anxious to leave the venue and indifferent to the reporter's aspiring agenda, Jack saw an opportunity to have some fun at his former lecturer's expense. Playing devil's advocate, the young man unleashed his wicked sense of humour, answering with a dead straight face:

"I'm afraid he isn't who he says he is. Neil Peterson lied to the audience today. His name is actually John Thomas; he hasn't officially changed it yet to my knowledge. It's an ongoing legal process though, which would explain his flushed expression. I just don't like people being deceived and talked down to, you know?"

Jack continued to explain to Hector how he felt that the event was in danger of becoming a farcical ego trip and that it needed to be opened up to the people. In a hilarious turn of events, due to Jack's eloquent opinion, the inexperienced reporter mistook his satirical opening for fact.

As Hector frantically scribbled down notes, Jack saw an opening in the horde of people at the door. Quickly excusing himself from Hector's presence, Jack made his way out of the building to buy his friends a well-earned drink.

Once he managed to escape the Town Hall entrance,

Jack found himself being accosted once again. However, this time it was by the local news team who had been covering the event. They had been waiting to interview him. Refreshed by the cool breeze after escaping the cramped confines of the crowded Town Hall, Jack felt less pressured and agreed to make a quick comment regarding the event, before meeting his friends at the pub.

A short way across town, Ginger sat at home recovering from her weakened condition, switching between thinking about the political excitement of the day and what kind of a cover story she should come up with if her boss saw her on T.V. Whatever repercussions may come from it, the event had definitely made her day more interesting and given her a lot more to think about than if she'd been cooped up in an office all day.

Before she knew it, 6 o'clock came round. It was time for her to face the music and watch the news. As a result of the anxiety which had manifested itself about being caught out, she had forgotten that she had witnessed a news story unfold before her very eyes earlier that day.

The news program covered the entire county. However, as it was a quiet day for news in that area of England, the story had earned itself an unprecedented 15 minutes of television time. Fortunately, Ginger had escaped being captured on camera.

Once she was satisfied she'd escaped the media's watchful eye, Ginger was able to give Jack's interview her full attention, through her relic of a television.

"As I said before, there are plenty of students who could have done a better job. But I have to say, I'm grateful it played out the way it did because I appreciated being able to engage with the community on a deeper level."

Jack's interview came to a close as the broadcast moved on to the regional weather.

Ginger still didn't know what to think; the only thing she was certain of was that the event had distracted her from the mundane mandatory task of going to work. A part of her felt drawn to Jack; his enigmatic presence at the town hall and free-spirited attitude resonated with her. She started to feel as though she had become trapped. Ginger's self-sufficient, full time working lifestyle had resulted in her spending almost every weekend in her pyjamas in front of the television.

Within a few hours, Ginger came to the realisation that, despite supporting herself, she felt unfulfilled.

After an exhausting review of the situation, she came to the conclusion he was a virtual stranger and it had just been an extremely unusual day. Her emotions drained and overcome with fatigue, Ginger got changed into her dressing gown, and unwound with some relaxing music and hot chocolate before an early night.

Meanwhile, on the outskirts of town, Hector Diamond was writing up his article for the following day's newspaper. He was including Jack's comment about the soon to be infamous John Thomas, still unaware of the joke and reporting it as fact.

Hector was eager to get his scoop in the paper to impress his superiors. Due to the last minute nature of printing, Hector's mistake remained undetected. This would be his second published story for the paper , and his first big mistake.

Jack was having a celebratory drink with a few of his mates down at his local pub.

"See, I knew, with your help, I could open people's eyes to the stupidity they're teaching these simpletons."

Jack laughed as he bought a round for his friends in the security and sound teams who had been overseeing the event earlier that day. The group were happy at what their friend had accomplished and were each proud to be a part of it.

As Jack turned back to the bar to collect his drink, a nondescript, middle-aged man with short grey hair and glasses stopped him.

"Well done young man, I haven't seen a show like that on the local news in quite some time." The man said with a cheeky smile.

Jack humbly thanked the man and offered to buy him a drink, inviting him to join his group of friends in the celebrations.

Chuckling, and with a tip of the head, the man declined before sharing some advice:

"You seem to be decent young men, but I've never been comfortable in groups. I feel I should forewarn you. There's no peace once you're in the public eye. I've seen people be consumed by it even when they were merely working behind the scenes. Whatever happens, don't let being the flavour of the month define who you are. There's more to you than the papers and T.V. programs could ever show, even if they were honest."

Jack felt he wanted to get to know the mysterious stranger more, however the time and the place didn't feel right, and he couldn't abandon his friends. Without hesitation, he responded:

"I'll definitely bear that in mind, what's your name?"

"Fred," the man replied, before bidding Jack goodnight and leaving the pub.

Shaking off the momentary concern Fred's words had caused him, Jack grabbed his drink and returned to the table to resume the laddish banter.

The next morning, Ginger awoke to the excruciating sound of her alarm clock. She felt a lot better in comparison to the previous day, so she resumed her morning routine of getting ready and setting off for work. On her way through town she passed a corner shop, where she discovered Jack Andrews was still the talk of the town. Glancing over the headlines she hurried on to work, determined to get there early to make up for the previous day's absence.

Once she arrived at the office, her shoes clip-clopped

on the smooth, clean concrete flooring. The cool air conditioning brushed the back of her neck as she made her way to her desk. Surprised at feeling so fresh, she sat down to start her day's work. Logging on to her computer Ginger updated herself on what she had missed.

Out of the blue, the sound of a newspaper being slapped on her desk startled her.

"Miss Taylor, what are you doing there? That was yesterday when you were allegedly sick,"

her boss demanded, pointing to her picture in the paper. Frozen in an awkward silence that seemed to last forever, Ginger then turned to face her boss.

"Don't even bother trying to explain, disciplinary action here we come!"

Ginger's boss sniped as he strutted off upstairs to his office, leaving his anxious employee to ponder her fate.

After further inspecting the paper, she realised it had printed two pictures of her. One showed her sitting behind Jack and, even more concerning, one with Jack looking on as she left during his speech. The reporter Hector Diamond had even put a caption under the picture:

"Potential girlfriend leaving during boyfriend's big moment?"

Outraged at the implication, Ginger rang the Rockshore Messenger to complain. At the printing office, the chief editor Ted Lesley took the call and found himself apologising profusely. Moments after the call, Ted ordered Hector into his office. Hector entered the room with confidence, smirking and assuming he would be praised for his latest story covering the Talk of the Town event.

"It's ten to nine in the morning and I've already had two telephone calls complaining about the report you've done. So you can wipe that grin right off your face, Diamond!"

Hector's face dimmed in horror as he heard his boss chastise his efforts in finding a scoop. Re-adjusting his tone, Ted swept his hand over his grey pompadour.

"I realise that you used to work for one of these gossip magazines where the wilder the story was, the more money you could make. But this is a well-respected news company, and it's an entirely different style of working. You can't write unconfirmed facts without repercussions. The girl in the picture isn't his girlfriend; she doesn't even know him. More embarrassingly though Neil Peterson is NOT called John Thomas! That's a slang phrase…. Look it up. Surely you can tell the difference between a serious fact and an upstart kid having a laugh at his former teacher's expense! You're going to have to write an apology. Humble pie tastes better if you learn from it. So let this be a lesson to you."

Hector apologised to his boss and took his advice on board; however, under the surface of his remorse lay a deep resentment towards Jack Andrews. Although he had been deceived, Hector was unable to see that his unbridled ambition had caused him to be reckless in his reporting. Instead, Hector placed the blame solely on Jack as he stared at his smiling picture in the paper, filled with vengeance.

As the day progressed and the late morning sun became more visible, Jack emerged from his alcohol-induced slumber. His eyes were rudely awakened by the harsh rays of the sun shining through his friend's blinds. With a heavy hangover, he sat up from the bizarre position he had slept in on his mate's sofa. With a mouth dryer than a desert storm, Jack nursed his sore head as he got up off the couch. Carefully manoeuvring around his passed out friends, dazed and confused, yesterday's hero plodded into the kitchen to get a glass of water. Gazing out the kitchen window of his friend's third story Jacksville flat, his bleary eyes drifted around the estate gardens.

He felt the irritating vibration of his phone go off in his pocket. Retrieving his phone, he discovered he'd received a text reminding him about kickboxing that night.

"Crap, I've actually got to exercise like this?!"

Jack said to himself, realising he faced high-intensity physical training despite being heavily hung-over. Concocting a half-baked plan to himself, he left the flat in search of an energy drink to set him right for the day.

Ginger had escaped work; her angry boss had become increasingly angrier at her previous day's absence as the day went on. Never one to take abuse, Ginger told her now former boss what he could do with his job and himself. On her way home, she took her usual stroll through Jacksville.

To her somewhat surreal surprise, she saw Jack staggering up the street. She didn't know if it was him or not, but someone from across the street took his picture on their mobile phone. Jack was in no condition to notice; however, he did recognise Ginger from the day before. He smiled as he wished her good morning. Never one to be rude, she greeted him back, asking why he was looking so rough.

Although he was hung-over, Jack's answer still reflected the controversial insight he had displayed the day before:

"Just because I'm interested in engaging with my community at Talk of the Town, doesn't mean I don't enjoy a night on the town. What brings you down to Jacksville?"

Stressed out about her argument with her boss, Ginger realised she didn't have a lot of people to talk to in her life. Taking the rare opportunity to share her grievance, she began to tell Jack about quitting her job due to unfair treatment from her boss. She asked him what he was doing for the day.

Jack took a moment to soak in the fresh air to soothe his throbbing head before replying:

"My plans are to get a sugar-saturated energy drink to give me enough juice to get through the day, and then I have to go get beat up tonight. But if you happened to be free in about an hour's time, we could get to know each other better."

Ginger seemed taken aback by the relaxed manner in which he had just invited her, a random stranger, out for the day. She also couldn't believe the spontaneous nature her day was taking in comparison to the rest of her year. Satisfied with her response, Jack looked at his phone, checking the time

"Hmm, meet you back here in about an hour and a half?"

Ginger nodded, and the two went their separate ways.

Jack went to the shop on his way home.

Home was an interesting concept for Jack; he had formed many contacts throughout his life and cultivated many different friendships with many different people. He had moved away from his parents when he was very young and had several adopted families.

He had five different addresses, each with different belongings and outfits stored. He'd decided what he wanted to wear for the day so he wandered down to the Mason's house which was in the next section of town, drinking his energy drink as he went.

The Masons were one of Jack's first foster families. Running away from a number of homes at a young age, Jack had broken a lot of family's hearts. However, he had reconnected with Sue and Dominic Mason at a later date and apologised to them; they knew he was a free spirit at heart and forgave him his wandering ways.

They just wanted to know he was safe. Jack respected that and sent them a text each night saying goodnight. On his arrival, the house was empty. He put his phone on charge, showered and changed into his summer smart casual wear. Although he looked good, he felt something was missing from his outfit.

Only half an hour had passed, so he borrowed his foster father's watch and left the house again. This time he jogged to his first girlfriend's house. He hadn't resided there for several years; however, he was still close friends with her and had adopted her as a surrogate sister. He mainly used their house for storage of his most prized possessions.

Knocking on their door, Gemma answered.

"Jack! What brings you here today?"

He explained his situation and quickly went up to the loft to retrieve his accessories. Jack valued Gemma's opinion as a friend, a sister and, in this case, a stylist. Jack tried on various different bracelets and watches that he'd accumulated over the years. Each item had a sentimental back story to it signifying how varied his life had been. Jack reassured Gemma:

"Look sis, it doesn't matter which one you think goes. I've got to wear one because it will give me a story to break the ice with."

After picking out a large dark leather bracelet that complimented his outfit, he set off, thanking Gemma as he went. The bracelet had been given to him by another one of his surrogate families who had sent it to him from overseas as a gift for helping them out. At this point, he had 20 minutes left. Jack sprinted back to the Mason's and dropped off Mr Mason's watch before applying himself with deodorant and collecting his halfway charged phone.

Observing his perfectly windswept hair on the way out of the house, Jack felt reassured that he was going to make the best impression he could.

With 5 minutes to spare Jack arrived back at the meeting place. Peering around the still quiet streets of Jacksville, he sniffed and checked under his armpits. To his delight the deodorant hadn't worn off. Casually checking the time, the minutes slowly progressing, Jack started to wish he'd given her some sort of contact details just in case she couldn't make it. He usually enjoyed the mystery of leaving things to chance; however, there was something about this girl that made Jack regret his decision.

Contemplating a respectable time limit for him to cut his losses and walk away, Jack stood pondering why he felt so strongly about a girl he'd only just met. All of a sudden his train of thought was interrupted by the approaching sound of hurried footsteps.

"Ugh, sorry I'm late. I'm not normally late."

Ginger gasped as she reached Jack, panting for breath.

Amused at the effort she had put into meeting him, Jack reassured her with a smile:

"It's not every day you quit your job and meet a stranger within a couple of hours of knowing them. I hope. Running on a day like this is thirsty work; do you want to grab a drink?"

Recovering from her unplanned sprint, Ginger nodded in approval and the two set off on their way to the local shop. As spontaneous as the day was, Jack had formed a brief plan of what they could do with the beautiful weather that awaited them.

Meanwhile, back at the stuffy offices of the local paper, Hector schemed and steamed away at his keyboard. Trying to concoct a legally bulletproof angle that would dethrone this ascending hero, he sat cooking in the rays of the sun and his own resentment.

He was among the few people in the building that wanted to be there on such an inviting day. However, he hadn't looked out of the window long enough to notice it. Hector had several applications open on his computer, and he sat, waiting like a sadistic fisherman, until something popped up on a social media site. His vengeful eyes gleamed as he discovered a picture post capturing Jack's sorry state from a couple of hours earlier.

Seizing the opportunity, he contacted the user asking permission to use his post. To his delight, he received a positive response within minutes. Upon further photo analysis, Hector realised that the picture of a hungover Jack was in Jacksville. Knowing that the area was notorious for crime and racial discrimination, Hector scowled as he strategically placed the image and prepared his opening headline:

"Home town hero?"

Oblivious to the backlash developing, Jack and Ginger were enjoying a gentle stroll, with the whole town at their disposal for entertainment. Pondering their options, Jack enquired:

"When was the last time you went down to the funfair?"

Ginger had to take a few moments to reflect on when she had last been there. Though she hadn't realised it, they were already on their way. She finally recalled that she hadn't been there since she was 11. On further reflection, she'd forgotten there even was a funfair in town.

After Ginger had finished her account of her last time at the fair, she turned the question back on Jack. He recalled it was in the latter part of the previous autumn, when he had won an air hockey tournament at the arcade.

The two new friends drew nearer to the seafront, admiring the vibrant greenery the passing trees and bushes provided in the light of the fresh summer sun.

It was still term time and the children hadn't been released from their schools yet, so the atmosphere was considerably quieter than Ginger had ever seen it before.

Through the constricting institutions of both education and work environments, Ginger had forgotten a number of places and activities that the town had to offer. She found her senses all being refreshed through rediscovering her hometown with her new found companion.

The positive vibes in the air had dissolved any doubts either of them may have had about getting to know each other. Consequently, the small talk started to evolve, allowing them to get a true sense of their respective characters and how they could relate and fit into one another's lives.

"So what did make you crash that debate yesterday? And how did you manage to pull that all off?" Ginger asked.

Pre-empting the question, Jack smiled answering:

"For starters, one thing that is absolutely crucial to living the way I do is having a lot of friends. I knew a bunch of guys working behind the scenes at that event. I knew the security team, the sound team and a number of members of the crowd who were biting their tongues. Some of them wouldn't have spoken out of fear, some because they felt educationally outmatched, but all of the people I knew in that crowd resented what they were hearing. "

Ginger was surprised at how many people Jack knew, and how many people had helped facilitate his stunt from behind the scenes. She was also impressed with the tenacity with which he cared for their feelings. Jack continued to answer the other part of her question:

"My motives weren't entirely selfless, I must confess. As mentioned at the event, I used to be on the politics course at Rockshore University, with the hope of becoming a more informed, functioning member of society. Sadly I learned this would not be the case at the outset of my educational career. I discovered that although they said there were no right or wrong answers, the people in power were extremely biased. Basically, if you weren't singing from their hymn sheet, you wouldn't be heard at all. I soon realised it was a reflection on how modern society works. If someone makes the people in charge happy, that person will get somewhere. If that person happens to throw someone else under the bus while they're doing it, they'll look even better."

Taken aback by Jack's answer, Ginger asked what had given him that sort of opinion. She felt that everyone should and could be heard in politics.

Taking her question on board Jack sighed:

"That's the way I thought it should be too. Sadly, I don't believe it to be the case anymore. People are just itching to prove their superiority over one another. Sometimes to the extent that winning a pointless debate becomes more important than the issue itself."

Ginger found what Jack was saying hard to believe. However, she could sense through the frustration in his voice that he was speaking from experience.

The conversation eventually dwindled off politics and on to their life experiences. As they approached the funfair, Ginger heard the familiar sounds of the fair and the nostalgic '90s Euro-pop music from her childhood. She could feel her face lighting up as her subconscious skimmed through memories of her and her parents on the Illuminator rollercoaster and the breath-taking view from the Ferris wheel.

The sight of the sky blue lights on the wheel and the luminous purple lights on the rollercoaster cast her mind back to a time where she was freed from the mind-numbing obligations of full-time office work.

Jack could sense her joy as he looked deeper into her freckled face, which was seasoned with excitement. This became increasingly apparent once the smell of warm candy-floss re-entered her nose for the first time in over a decade.

"Looks like someone's just turned 11 again," Jack laughed.

Serotonin flowing through her mind, Ginger giggled like she hadn't done in years.

Although no logical person would dream of walking out of a job the way she had earlier that day, she found herself genuinely happy at that moment, no matter what repercussions were to follow.

After her natural nostalgic high had passed, Ginger started to wonder what Jack did for a living.

He was dressed quite smartly, but she remembered he

had looked rather scruffy the previous day. Though he was well spoken and articulate, he didn't seem like he wanted to show it. Ginger found it very difficult to categorise him into a social class or even a basic stereotype because of his contradictory appearances.

Before she knew it, Jack had bought her a stick of candy-floss and an ice-cream for himself. Giving up on her unspoken guesswork, she asked him what his job was.

Jack made a start on his ice-cream while he pondered the question, listening to the '90s pop music as the suspense became visible on Ginger's face. After a few long seconds, he finally responded:

"It's a complicated state of affairs."

Ginger was outraged at Jack's evasive answer and she slapped him on the arm as he chuckled at the disapproving look on her face. Amused at his antics, Ginger pushed on:

"Seriously! You heard all about my job. What do you do?"

Jack stopped himself laughing long enough to give a serious answer, as he licked his ice-cream here and there to stop it from dripping:

"I'm a traveller. I'm not employed, so I don't let a company put a value on my time and I sure as hell don't kick any money up to the government. I just do favours for people and they do favours for me."

Trying to comprehend what she had just heard, Ginger asked how he managed to do what he was doing. Still enjoying his ice-cream, Jack answered:

"I'm officially homeless, but in a sense I have more homes than the fat cats have houses."

Sensing the confusion and curiosity throbbing through Ginger's inquisitive mind, Jack elaborated on his past:

"I grew up here, but because of my heritage and accent, I never fitted in. I hated my school, the cruelty from both pupils and teachers. I wasn't particularly academically gifted, so I used to run away. I'd ask the right people for train fares, usually elderly people who looked like kind-hearted grandparents.

The authorities always picked me up, but after this had happened a few times, they took me away from my uncaring parents. Over time I was placed with incredibly kind families, abusive families, all sorts, but I never felt at home in a home no matter how nice it was. In academic terms, I was an ungradable student.

But what the schools I went to couldn't possibly pick up on was that I was always learning. I'd be living life, watching situations, talking to people, learning things that the kids in the classes couldn't. I caught up with the curriculum through different ways and got myself up to university, the pinnacle of British education. All I found there were a number of people who had become too self-assured because they'd done as they were told and had been praised for being what they were supposed to.

What I learned was the value of being true to myself and the people I care for. I survived the streets of Britain in many different cities, alone as an uneducated child. Any paedophile, psychopath, stray animal or vehicle could have mentally scarred or killed me. But fate seemed to protect me to an extent, and I did what the vast majority of this society couldn't do, alone. I can achieve anything with the right friends, family and contacts."

Ginger hadn't heard anything like this before outside of films or books. She couldn't believe how alone this man had been from such a young age. An uncontainable, free spirit who had adapted and thrived in this world in a way she couldn't possibly understand.

She felt a tear trickle down her cheek. Although he still hadn't explained the logistics of how he achieved such an impressive feat of independence, she found herself at a loss for words.

Part of her envied him as his life seemed so much more interesting than hers. Noticing the stunned silence and the amalgamation of emotions swarming through Ginger's mind, Jack tried to lighten the mood:

"At least you haven't accused me of making it all up. A lot of people do… I'm not by the way."

Ginger could see in his eyes that his account was genuine; however, she was stumped for conversation after such a shocking revelation. Jack had dealt with this before while trying to explain himself to the Masons', among other families, over the years.

Gradually, as the day went on, Ginger gained more of an understanding about Jack and how he was grateful for his journey and where it had taken him in life. If there was one thing he'd developed through his storied past, it was an eclectic sense of humour.

In a less positive environment, Hector Diamond had made substantial progress towards his calculating, character assassinating article on Jack. He was feeling increasingly vindicated with each sentence he constructed. He had even credited the photo to the young man who had permitted him to use it and took a statement, claiming that he was "staggering up the street half cut at 11 o'clock that morning."

As much as that could be manipulated into changing the public's image of their new local hero, Hector knew that it wouldn't be enough to completely destroy his character.

He once again contacted the young man who had taken the photo and encouraged him to keep an eye out for more of the same kind of pictures of Jack to assist him in his expose. Even if he had to wait until the next day he was going to have his revenge on the upstart who had publicly outwitted him.

Hector Diamond didn't even register in Jack's memory, which was unsurprising with the fast-moving pace of his never-ending adventure-filled lifestyle. At that point Jack and Ginger were having the time of their lives once again, admiring the view of the city from a cart on the Ferris wheel.

Jack hoped the view from the wheel would distract Ginger from what he had told her. In the distance they saw a helicopter hovering over the city.

They speculated what sort of a helicopter it could be and why it might be up there. Laughing and joking, they took in the other sights while the cart reached the highest point of the ride. Eventually their eyes met.

Jack could feel his heart rate begin to increase as their souls were staring directly into one another. Ginger's lips began to quiver as though she wanted to say something but was taken by the moment.

Eventually she managed to whisper:

"I'm sorry, I'm not into guys."

Jack averted his gaze with a smile of understanding:

"No need to apologise, I invited you out to get to know you better and I feel that I've gained a friend. I couldn't ask for more than that."

Ginger sighed in relief at Jack's understanding and reached out to hug him tightly. At that moment, Jack could smell the strong scent of lavender in her perfume. A smell that would trigger this memory for many years to come.

Concluding their ride on the wheel, they spent an hour or so gaming at the arcade. Ginger couldn't help but wonder how Jack could afford to do so much. As they were shooting virtual monsters with colourful electronic guns, Ginger finally asked him.

"Best way to describe it is pocket money. Hang on, I'll explain after we kill this plant monster!"

Jack shouted over the hideous noises the arcade machine was making.

Once the game had ended he continued:

"All my friends are rich in different ways and they've all got incredible personalities. I do favours for people and they pay me. Sometimes I'll do the favours myself and other times I'll have another friend do it in payment for my services to them. It works out like any other business relationship. Except it runs solely on trust and goodwill rather than financial currencies, the value of which changes by the day."

Ginger laughed:

"How is that any different from the mob?"

Jack laughed admitting there wasn't much difference, but he explained that the mob was run like a family, and that in amongst the brutality that it was famous for there were family values too.

Amused and slightly bemused, Ginger commented:

"You are one strange dude! I don't know how you can live on luck and rely so heavily on others."

Jack's face glistened with contentment as he answered:

"It's funny, I'm not always rich. Whatever I have in my pockets is mine to spend, I don't have a bank account and I don't keep track of it at all to be honest. Sometimes I don't have two coins to rub together. But, I'm never without a roof over my head, I never miss a meal and I'm never alone unless I want to be. I guess I'm blessed to have such great people in my life. Truth be told, no matter what I do for them I can never repay them properly for the happiness they bring to my life."

Ginger felt herself being inspired by her new found friend and thought she too was blessed by fate, to bestow such a unique and positive young man upon her world.

She came to once again question everything she'd come to believe through the media, realising that people must be judged on more than what they do for a living, and that their quality of life isn't always dependant on their net worth.

At first she was fearful of the uncertain concept of this young man's life, but before her stood a confident, well-nourished, positive young man who had built himself up from nothing, due only to his ability to get on with people and willingness to help them out.

In an outburst of raw happiness, Ginger exclaimed:

"I'm so happy to have met you!"

Returning the compliment, Jack invited her to go for a walk along the seafront. Accepting his invitation with pleasure, Ginger left the arcade and they headed past the harbour and down the esplanade. Looking over at the blend of both sand and stones the beach presented, Ginger stopped Jack in his tracks picking up a sizable stone:

"You've brought me down to the beach for the first time in I don't know how long. It's really quiet. There's no way we're not throwing stones in the sea."

At that precise moment, the mischievous photographer from earlier rode past undetected on a push bike with his hood up. In a split second, he managed to capture a shot which totally misrepresented the moment.

The image showed a look of surprise on Jack's face, the stone in Ginger's hand and her other hand placed across Jack's chest, making it look as if she was threatening him.

Racing off as he had arrived, the aspiring street paparazzi had fulfilled what his unacquainted employer had encouraged him to do. Pulling up out of sight, he sent his picture to Hector's e-mail address.

Back in the stuffy office of the devious Mr Diamond, Hector cracked his knuckles in satisfaction, adding the picture to his project. His shirt was sticking to his back with the sweat he'd worked up typing Jack's fictitious dirt sheet.

Though the man was taking great pleasure in his parasitic work, he was blissfully ignorant of the enjoyment Jack and Ginger were experiencing back at the beach.

Before they knew it, dusk approached and Jack had to go to his kickboxing class. Unfortunately, Ginger had to venture back to her reality of trying to find a new job online. However, they exchanged numbers and she agreed to meet him afterwards for a drink.

Although she needed the security of a new job, Ginger was enjoying the welcome change Jack's company had already brought into her life.

Going their separate ways, they both felt a renewed sense of happiness, and they ventured towards their future as the sun began to set. Jack set off to his nearest home to retrieve his fitness gear. Thanks to the unpronounceable ingredients of his energy drink and the compelling company Ginger had provided for the day, Jack had forgotten all about his hangover.

Retrieving his equipment, he set off back to Jacksville to meet his kickboxing friend. Jack's friend Marty had been going to this kickboxing class for a number of years, but Jack had only just joined.

Marty was a loyal friend of Jack's; the two had helped each other through many a street fight over the years. However, Jack had devoted time to catching up on his education in later life and worked through the gaps seeking knowledge from tutors, authors and a number of other people he had met with different backgrounds. This enabled Jack to progress through the education system and achieve a degree, opening up various different social avenues for him.

Marty on the other hand had continued to lead a rough and ready life. He was known to the police for various public order offences and fights around the town.

Marty was honest at heart and was true to his friends above all else, which Jack respected. He would sometimes end up in fights due to other people's hostility about his rugged appearance. After years of experiencing this, Marty would often be looking for hostility in others, and at times could be pre-emptively hostile himself.

After a brief catch-up, the two long-time friends made their way to Marty's local kickboxing class. Jack knew that this kickboxing class was run by local skinheads from around the Jacksville area. However, unlike the people in his old schools, they had made him feel welcome and hadn't judged him because of his voice.

The town had branded all the residents of Jacksville who fitted the stereotypical profile of a white skinhead as racist thugs. However, in the few months that Jack had known the kickboxing class and the many years he had known Marty, they had not demonstrated any racist or discriminatory behaviour. Jack had witnessed several ethnic members of the community being welcomed into the kickboxing class, including a Rockshore University student named Adric, who was from Jamaica.

Adric was a strong athletic young man who instantly took to the class. He enjoyed channelling his pent-up frustrations with university life into physical combat. Although Rockshore University provided sports societies, the fees were extortionate and Adric far preferred the company of the Jacksville Club. Furthermore, Adric was comfortable enough with his peers within the group to engage in banter with them.

Jack was partnered with Adric as the two were both reasonably new to the class. Jack was exhausted and his stamina had reached a low point.

Adric caught him with a kick to the face, giving him a black eye. The fight was stopped and the two laughed it off like true sportsmen.

Following the session, the Jacksville kickboxing class embarked on their weekly visit to the Town Cryer pub (aka the TC). The TC was located in the town square and was at the heart of the city's nightlife. By this time, it was nine o'clock This was usually when the night-time economy came to life. There were around 12 members of the kickboxing class, and it was a very rare occasion that one of them missed the pub after the class. Tonight was not one of those times; 11 of them were there, and one would arrive later.

Adric had decided to go home and get changed. Although the other members of the class were happy to go out in the clothes they had brought, Adric took great pride in his appearance and always wanted to look and feel his best on a night out. He lived within 10 minutes of the establishment so he would join them shortly after.

The TC was reasonably quiet, though that was bound to change throughout the evening.

Apart from a few random social groups and the kickboxing class there was a large table of students which looked like some sort of university society's social meeting.

A large bald older man waited by the bar; he stood out in the crowd because of his Hench physique, standing at 6'foot 6 inches tall. No-one in the bar was aware that the man was a historical national celebrity.

His name was Big Ben, an extremely popular British wrestler from decades ago. His fame had dwindled in time, which he had grown to enjoy.

As the kickboxing class piled into the large pub, the students started to notice them. Allister Benedict was amongst the students. His face dropped with contempt as he saw the skin-headed kickboxers enter the bar.

"Oh, here comes the urban Nazis and look who's with them. It's that bigot sympathiser from yesterday."

Allister exclaimed with disgust as he drew his peer's attention to the kickboxers. The other students joined Allister in his character assassination of the group at the bar.

With each snide comment made, Allister and his fellow students were getting more and more wound up. At the bar, Jack and Marty were having a great time with their friends. Due to the loud and rambunctious behaviour of the group, the other customers were becoming increasingly convinced of their stereotyped thuggish reputation.

At the other end of town, Hector was in communications with his anonymous photographer. After discovering Jack had attended a kickboxing class in Jacksville, he offered his spy a substantial reward for finding and picturing Jack with the "racist Jacksville residents". To his delight, Hector found out that his spy was already in the camp. He could see tension mounting at the students' table, so he thought he'd wait for the right moment to take the incriminating photograph.

A mysterious girl arrived at the venue; like the large wrestler, she too stood out from the crowd. However, this was mainly due to her pale complexion and dyed black and sapphire hair. She also stood out with her unique style of clothing compared to the other customers. Dressed in a long dark dress, with a black leather corset, her outfit was completed with a distinctive silk cardigan, which looked like it had been crafted somewhere in Europe.

The girl's outlandish appearance was matched only by the aura of confidence she carried with her as she strutted through the growing crowd at the entrance.

Soon after the arrival of the eye-catching Goth, Adric returned to the venue dressed in a suit jacket, white shirt and jeans. Dressed to kill and out for a thrill, Adric snuck up on a couple of his kickboxing comrades. Allister and a couple of his peers approached the bar, speculating on and scrutinizing the Jacksville residents' behaviour. One of the other kickboxers realised Adric had turned up so he greeted his friend, bellowing across the bar "Tambourine."

Adric's nickname within the group; he welcomed this nickname as it was a reference to his ringtone, discovered when his phone went off during one of his first sessions. Although it was an inside joke between Adric and his fellow kickboxers; Allister and his student friends assumed it was a racial slur.

Filled with self-righteous rage, Allister signalled for more of his university peers to join him at the bar to confront the skinheads over their misperceived racially insensitive behaviour.

Back at the students' table, one of the student's rants about the idiocy of Christianity was interrupted as they saw Allister's signal. Sensing trouble in the air, a couple of well-built members of the Rockshore University boxing society downed their pints and readied themselves to help Allister on his noble political quest.

Jack felt his pocket vibrate as his phone went off. Excusing himself from the growing crowd in the bar, he went out to answer it. It was Ginger who, having just arrived, was waiting for him outside.

As Jack left, Marty and another kickboxing friend were waiting to be served next to Big Ben. Their attention was caught by Allister further up the bar confronting Adric's skinhead friend.

"I'm absolutely disgusted with your racist attitude to this poor young man. He's from my university and I refuse to have some low life racist scum like you disrespect him!"

Allister exclaimed.

To his utter amazement, Adric intervened:

"What's your problem? We're having a joke. I make fun of his bald head; he makes fun of my ringtone. Get your head out your arse, man!"

Allister averted his gaze to the alcohol-soaked laminated flooring: flustered and humiliated, he made his way back to the table. Meanwhile, outside there was a friendlier environment as Jack greeted Ginger.

"What happened to your face?"

She enquired with concern. Jack told her how Adric had caught him with a decent hit while he was off guard. Jack couldn't wait to introduce her to him. Unfortunately, neither of them could have predicted what was about to unfold inside the Town Cryer.

Back in the bar, Allister was still seething with anger. As he regrouped with his fellow students from the boxing society, the mysterious gothic girl had slid to the front of the queue which had built up around the bar, caught the bar steward's attention and ordered a drink. Marty and his friend were angry at this as she had undercut them.

"Oi mate we've been waiting for almost 10 minutes and you served her before us!"

Marty exclaimed in irritation. Adding fuel to his fire, the arrogant young lady smiled at her self-satisfaction:

"I should be served first; I'm practically royalty in my own country."

Never one to take well to self-centred people, Marty replied:

"I don't care if you're the bloody queen of England, if you're in our country you wait your turn."

As Marty reprimanded the overbearing young lady, Allister and his peers overheard him and moved to confront Marty and his friend.

"How dare you talk to her like that, you misogynistic, racist scumbag! I'm sick of you ignorant Jacksville thugs!"

Encouraged by Allister's lead, his boxing cronies confronted two of the other kickboxing class members and Big Ben, mistaking him for one of their gang.

Big Ben had been keeping to himself and had not paid much attention to the dispute. However, the irritated students continued to pursue their misguided assumptions.

"Look lads, I've nothing to do with any of this, I'm having a pint in my local and I'm almost three times your age. I'm old enough to be all of your grandfathers, especially by this town's standards." The weary wrestler explained.

Unconvinced, the boxers continued to accuse them:

"Don't try and get out of it now, you've probably been a racist for years! You people are a disgrace!"

Becoming disconcerted with the escalating anger surrounding the bar, the mysterious lady retreated, heading back to her table of one.

"See you've made her feel like she had to leave now!"

One of the boxers claimed, squaring up to Marty. The bar was quite crowded at this point as people had filtered in as the night had progressed.

Big Ben started to feel claustrophobic and trapped.

"Okay, enough is enough. I'm going now; you kids enjoy yourselves."

He sighed and turned away as he tried to make his exit.

One of the boxers pushed Marty as the tensions built.

Marty fell into Big Ben's back, causing him to accidentally knock a glass off the bar. Shaken by the excruciating sound of the glass shattering, and thinking that the boxer had shoved him from behind, Big Ben turned round in anger. With one hand on Marty and another on one of the boxers he shoved them both back, sending them hurtling into the other patrons at the bar.

The other boxer tried to punch Big Ben but due to the amount he had drunk, his reflexes had slowed. Big Ben pre-emptively slapped him on the chest with an open hand; the single blow sent the young man to the floor and left him gasping for breath.

The backlash caused by the other people at the bar falling, led to several other fights breaking out within the group, and before long a mass brawl was in progress. Furious, the gargantuan former wrestler barged his way out of the pub.

Outside, Ginger and Jack had started to notice the affray inside the pub as the bouncers on the door radioed for back up. Even the locals had started to get involved; even old war veterans who missed the thrill of conflict had joined the fray.

"What the hell's going on in there?" Jack called out in concern.

Ginger could see the young man from earlier with his camera phone out, filming the escalating riot. She started to realise that if Jack went back in there, it could be manipulated to look like he was one of the agitators.

"You can't go back in there, Jack! If you're arrested or you're said to be in there, they'll hang you out to dry in the press and everything you achieved the other day will be undone. You're not this person Jack!"

Ginger pleaded as she grabbed his arms; increasing panic and fear grew in Jack's eyes:

"They're my friends. I can't leave them in there. The press is full of lies anyway!"

As he was arguing his case to Ginger, they were

interrupted as Marty had thrown one of the students out of the window. The brawl continued as it spilled out into the street. Within seconds, people from other clubs started to get involved and violent outbursts now infected the whole street. Within moments it had escalated into a riot. Even Jack was shocked at what was transpiring before his eyes. He soon realised nothing he could do would make this dangerous situation any better.

"Alright, let's get out of here."

Jack agreed, knowing the only thing he could do was to get Ginger to safety.

The pair hurried off through the town square, just as the sound of police sirens drew nearer. Once they had escaped the vicinity they both sighed with relief, looking down at the cobbled path which led back through the dead streets of the town centre. The adrenaline started to wear off and the two embraced each other, thankful that they were both safe after witnessing such chaos.

"Thank goodness we got out of there in time! Those Jacksville thugs are out of control."

Ginger exclaimed.

Jack drew away in despair explaining:

"Look, I don't know the ins and outs of what happened in there. All I know is those boys wouldn't have started a fight without a damn good reason or out of self-defence. They're old-school, if they were going to fight, they'd have taken it outside."

Ginger scoffed in disbelief:

"Yeah, we saw them take it out to the street. Through a pane glass window! It's a good job you didn't get caught on camera going back in there, and what makes you think so highly of them?"

Wiping the sweat from his brow and adjusting the straps on his backpack, Jack began to explain:

"Because I know them as individuals and as friends;

they don't always choose their words as carefully and kowtow to the norms of civilised society. But, you know where you stand with them. I didn't leave them because I was worried about being caught there.

The truth is the way the public sees me doesn't matter.

I don't... the media will either forget about me or shoot me down one day anyway. My life revolves around friends and no flavour of the month story will affect the relationships I've cultivated over the years. If Marty gets the book thrown at him for putting the window in and branded as something he's not in the paper, it won't take away the years we've stood by each other's side; that man is a brother to me."

At this stage, Ginger didn't know whether to feel inspired or shocked at his naivety:

"Then why did you leave them there?"

Jack's smile slowly returned to his face as he answered:

"Because you're my friend too. They can take care of themselves in a scrap; none of them needed my help in that department. It was more important to keep you safe and out of harm's way. The irony is if I do get accused of being involved in that riot, no one will know because the facts will be twisted in the media.

None of that matters to me though. It doesn't matter what gets put in the paper about me today or tomorrow, no one will care in the end. No article is able to paint a full picture of what happens in a day in someone's life. Times like we had today at the fair, where we could just have fun, two unchained spirits enjoying a moment that most people have never experienced outside of their short-lived childhoods. Meeting someone and getting to know them as a person and a friend, that's what matters to me."

With a nod of understanding from Ginger, Jack knew that he would be facing whatever the future held with one more loyal friend by his side.

S.A. BALLANTYNE

Sea-Side City

Night Coat Origins

Night Coat Origins

Cover photo sourced from:
Pexels

Originally uploaded by:
Isaac Weatherly

Recoloured by:
S.A. Ballantyne

NIGHT COAT ORIGINS:

A tense, thought-filled silence enveloped the tranquil, scented room; Raymond Adebayo patiently awaited his client's account of what had brought him to counselling.

Eventually, the troubled young man unburdened his soul:

"All the time you hear about people having their heart broken. But, somehow this feels worse.

Bloody hell, saying that out loud sounds arrogant,"

the young man stated, as his pain-filled piercing blue eyes met Raymond's, exposing the depths of torture his soul had endured. He paused for a moment to collect his thoughts. Raymond maintained a gentle attentive manner, allowing the young man to continue.

"I had to break my own heart to keep my sanity, but I still feel like my world has fallen apart."

Observing the exhaustion laced through the pale, sleep-deprived and weary face that sat before him, Raymond reflected:

"Sounds like you're carrying a number of burdens. Not only are you suffering the effects of ending a highly stressful relationship, which took a toll on your sanity, but you feel a reluctance to express this pain through a fear of sounding arrogant."

Breaking eye contact, Alex gazed around the room as he processed Raymond's perceptive prognosis. Scanning the beige room, he saw it was decorated with framed artwork, qualifications and inspirational quotes. He started to realise that he was judging himself because he felt a sense of inadequacy and failure in breaking up with his former girlfriend.

He had attended counselling to help him through his break up. Unfortunately, with his small town upbringing, Alex had become accustomed to keeping secrets so as not to draw negative attention to himself or his family.

As a result of this, Alex found it difficult to disclose information about his former relationship. Paradoxically, his reluctance to disclose information prevented him from being able to further explore his feelings to gain a deeper understanding of himself.

Alex spent the remainder of the session reflecting on what aspects of the relationship haunted him the most. Raymond could sense there were layers of underlying issues to explore. However, he also appreciated the importance of Alex being able to discuss his relationship problems without judgement or haste. Eventually, Raymond brought the session to a close. Alex slipped his arms through the sleeves of his open draped large winter coat, arose from the leather armchair and left the room.

Taking his leave, Alex reached into his sizable side pocket searching for his trusty fizzy drink. Despite the numerous health warnings, he had received from the outside world, these legal sugar highs were Alex's crutch through his hours of need. He walked down the cool empty corridor, swigging from his bottle like a sober drunkard. Once he had had his fix, Alex took out his old battered music player as he exited the main building. Yet another bleak, overcast day awaited him. Tuning into his deafening nu-metal music and tuning out his surroundings and thoughts, Alex made his way home.

While Alex was travelling back to his terrace house, his

father was planted, immovable, in his two-seater sofa. Derick Douglas used to be a doorman; however, after becoming a published author some years earlier, he had refrained from physical activity. Subsequently, his mass had expanded alongside his literary talents. Before he knew it, he weighed 26 stone. With the television on in the background and a note pad in his lap, the proud Scotsman was slumped in the sofa, snoring as he snoozed the afternoon away, with his spectacles resting halfway down his nose.

Concluding his uneventful journey, Alex was unaware that his father was at home. He entered the house, slamming the door behind him. With his music still blaring at top volume, Alex had sacrificed his judgement of volume. He would soon be rudely awoken from his trance; much like the noise of the door had rudely awoken his grizzled father from his slumber. Derick's eyes widened and his chest expanded as he bellowed in his strong Scottish accent:

"Agh, idiot boy! What are you doing?"

His father's overwhelming presence was enough to draw Alex's attention back to reality and face the consequences of his accidental lack of consideration. Taking his earphones out, Alex looked at the T.V then back at his father before addressing him:

"Sorry Dad, didn't realise you were sleeping. How has your day been?"

Satisfied with his son's apology, Derick stretched and yawned:

"Ah, fine boy, just watching crap daytime T.V and looking for inspiration for this new book of mine. What about yourself?"

Alex told his father about his appointment with Raymond, but before he could explain what they had discussed during the session, he was interrupted:

"Oh no, you're not still making a fuss about that wee vampire that was round here are you?

For goodness sakes man, pull yourself together and get laid or something."

Derick agonised, looking at his son's shaggy hair, gaunt face and abandoned appearance. In a futile attempt to make his father understand his feelings, Alex persisted in trying to justify the benefits of counselling. Unfortunately, he was quickly interrupted once again by his flustered father

"What a load of… I don't…. You know the problem? This generation's too over-sensitised to everything. You got caught up with the wrong girl; all of a sudden the world's going to bloody collapse! You were running around like a blue-arsed fly for months trying to make her happy and now you're moping around like a sleep-deprived zombie."

Inhaling deeply, Derick continued his unrelenting rant:

"It's been a month; you're a young man in the prime of your life at university! That's a month you're going to regret wasting when you're older."

Irritated by his father's lack of empathy and outraged by his apathy, Alex left the confines of the front room. He retreated to his neglected lair of depression, formerly known as his bedroom.

Derick's frustration was a product of concern for his son's wellbeing. Sadly, his hot-headed mentality and old-fashioned views prevented him from expressing it. Alex appreciated the anger that had flushed over him. It was far easier to feel that way than to be caught up in the emotional limbo in which he usually found himself. Once upstairs, he opened the door to his room. Alex's nose was assaulted by the smell of dust, perspiration and the variety of ready-made meals he had devoured throughout the week. Visibility in the room was poor, as always; a consequence of the curtains always being closed.

Stumbling into the room, he manoeuvred his way around the offensive obstacle course. Once he reached his bed, he threw himself down in a defeated heap. Staring into the crack of light showing between the curtains, the concept of time became lost in the abyss of his mind.

Downstairs, Derick had returned to his sofa, which had become moulded to his ample posterior. "What's a skinny young thing like that doing moping around when he could be having the time of his life? I'd swap with him any day of the week," he muttered to himself as he took his glasses off, contemplating what to do with the rest of his day.

For a brief moment he flicked through the channels expressing his displeasure at what passed for entertainment in modern times. Giving up, he went upstairs to see what films he hadn't watched.

During Derick's ascension of the stairs, he grimaced at the stench that was emitting from Alex's room. Derick made a detour in the hope of addressing the smell. Standing in the door way, the disgruntled father scanned the room. Alex was staring blankly into space as Derick perceived the collection of unwashed crockery which had accumulated:

"Are you trying to attract cockroaches or something? It's a miracle we're not infested! No wonder you're depressed, living up here in this dung heap!"

Outraged at the sight of Alex's room, Derick collected the dishes and left the room, slamming the door behind him with his free arm.

Derick's comments registered with Alex. The terrain of his habitat wasn't helping his state of grief. Alas, in his slumped and sorrowful state, he was currently unable to act upon it. Remaining in his trance, Alex's mind kept taking him back to the same places.

In the early days, before the problems started, he had never known such happiness. Ever since he moved down to Rockshore to stay with his father, it felt as though something was missing. His mother was moving from his home town to Winchester. At that time Alex had a decision to make, move away with his mother or move away to attend university. He wanted to attend university, but he was sceptical about accumulating a hefty student loan. After constant arguments with his mother, Alex didn't want to move to Winchester with her either. He wanted a fresh start on his own.

With this in mind, he decided to reconnect with his father and attend Rockshore University. Reducing the costs of university living and starting fresh in the Sea Side City gave Alex the best of both worlds.

New in town and new to the university lifestyle, Alex found it difficult to make friends. He didn't drink alcohol and he found that he didn't have much in common with the people he met. As a result of this, his social life was limited. Instead, Alex lost himself in his work, achieving commendable grades in his criminology course.

Unlike a lot of students, Alex's home away from home was the library. After a few months he adapted to the solitude of his lifestyle.

One day, while making notes on his second assignment, Alex's attentions were diverted from his studies. It felt as though an extrasensory force was drawing his attention away from his work. Scanning the quiet surroundings of the library, a young lady stood out from everyone else. There was an aura of confidence and allure in her presence which instantly attracted him to her. Within seconds, her eyes met his from across the room. Before long they became acquainted and Alex would experience a great change in his life. Although the relationship had only lasted a few months, the intense period of isolation and co-dependent conditioning had altered his life beyond recognition.

After an intense and vivid review of their experiences together, Alex's agonised mind began to feel lethargic. Unaware of how long he had been lying there, he drifted off to sleep from mental exhaustion.

Downstairs, Derick reflected on his comments to his son. Despite his gruff exterior, Derick was a caring father.

However, he never wanted to mollycoddle his son because he wanted him to be a strong independent man. Unsure of how to shake off his guilt, Derick spent the rest of the brisk October evening in the comfort of his living room, relaxing to jazz music from his childhood. Eventually, he too reminisced himself to sleep.

Sometime in the early hours of the morning Alex started to awaken. His sleep pattern had become disjointed, much like his thought processes. Even though he awoke at such an unusual time, Alex had an epiphany. He decided to focus on widening his social groups as he had come to realise how isolated he now was. This wasn't the first burst of clarity he had experienced during this period of emotional chaos, but this time he appreciated how it felt to be free from his torturous thought processes.

Arising from his slumber, he was surrounded by darkness. Alex turned on his bedside lamp. He looked at the clock to see what the time was. The view of his clock was obscured by a row of empty cans. With the combination of his mental clarity and the light his lamp provided, he realised two things. The first was his addiction to sugary drinks was growing out of control, evidenced by the unhealthy number of cans around his room.

Secondly, he realised that his room had become a reflection of the inner workings of his mind. Overflowing with all the wrong things, blocking a clear view of the outside world, obscuring the concept of time and making it impossible to reach what he was looking for. Rubbing his hazy eyes, Alex got out of bed. Stretching out and breathing in the stuffy air of his room, he removed a couple of cans to see the time.

"3:16?" Alex whispered to himself, dumbfounded that he had awoken at such a time.

Through his nocturnal habits, he had gone to bed late many a time. He had even stayed up past that time before. But never in his life had he awoken at 3 o'clock in the morning.

"What the hell do I do at this time? It's too early to clean; maybe I should have a crack at some of that coursework I've been avoiding,"

he thought to himself as he paced around his cluttered room.

Clearing himself a path, Alex made his way to his computer. Throwing the pile of clothes off his chair and onto his bed, he sat down and logged on.

The familiar sounds of his console starting up comforted him as he opened the curtains. His bedroom window was covered in condensation as it had not been open for almost a week. It was in the latter part of October and the temperatures outside were dropping. Nonetheless, Alex felt a need to release the negativity from his room. He lifted the handle to his window and with one firm push, the window clicked open. A soothing cold draft rushed into the room. It felt as though Alex was breathing for the first time again.

Appreciating his moment of freedom, he turned back to face his computer.

Suddenly, he felt an agonising rush of adrenaline shoot through his body directly from his heart. The unmistakable sapphire blue eyes of his ex-girlfriend Angelica locked onto his for what felt like an eternity. Having not been on his computer for a month, she was still his background picture. The very face he had dreaded seeing stared back, deep into his wounded soul.

Her long black and blue dyed hair and alluring mystique radiated confidence, even through the pixels of his computer screen. All the visual aspects he once associated with love and inner happiness had mutated to despair and self-loathing.

A few seconds later, the sickening feeling passed and he deleted the photograph. Through the situations he had endured with Angelica over the passing months, he came to realise it was best to avoid her and keep himself safe; for this reason he had cut all ties with her.

However, after each rational decision he made, he would find himself being haunted by his imagination while trying to process the new data he had received.

At the back of his mind, he knew in his heart he still loved her, but his survival instincts told him she was too dangerous.

The complications were created by his imagination, which had become his worst enemy, draining his energy through trying to think of a way to make things work between them and things he could have done differently. His imagination had turned her into his worst fear. This had stemmed from the complete loss of any contact with her after he had removed himself from a relationship in which he had seen her every day. Alex's mind had turned her into some sort of supernatural dominating force against which he was completely powerless.

Once again, he started to reflect on the various situations they had been through together….

"Bloody hell, you're up early! It's 6 o'clock in the morning!" Derick's booming voice interrupted Alex's excruciating and tedious train of thought.

"Aye, that's good. Now you can start tidying up this fly tip. You can close the window now too; it's bloody freezing this morning!" He continued, before slamming Alex's door.

Alex looked at his computer clock in disbelief, realising he had passed three hours lost in his thoughts. He sprang to his feet, closing the window. Alex's hands were almost purple with the cold. Putting on some warmer clothes, he made a start at clearing the junk out of his room.

After almost five hours, Alex's bedroom was finally tidy enough to be called habitable. All obstacles had been removed, his bedding had been changed, and the room hoovered and dusted.

Looking around with some pride at his morning's work, he couldn't help but notice his tattered appearance in the gleaming polished mirror.

Knowing he looked out of place in his new and improved tidy room and that it was time for a new and improved Alex, he removed himself from the room to make a start on his own resurrection.

Downstairs Derick had also made progress as he had started to write his next novel. It wasn't long before nature intervened though. Derick unpeeled himself from his sofa and waddled up to the toilet. To his utter annoyance, the bathroom was occupied

"Of all the times for the lazy bugger to be out of his bed!" The behemoth grouch muttered as he wandered up the corridor, waiting for the toilet to be vacated.

He passed Alex's room; Derick was pleasantly surprised with the results of his son's morning's work. The smell of pine polish and freshly hoovered carpet were complimented with tasteful hints of air freshener. Derick's mood was lightened with the visual and nasal refreshments of Alex's newly cleaned room.

At that moment, the bathroom door swung open and a cloud of steam emptied out of the doorway, revealing the new Alex. Derick's face lit up at the sight of his freshly-shaved, clean son.

"Well, well! Welcome back boy."

Derick applauded as his son re-emerged from the bathroom. "Now go and get your hair cut and let me in there,"

he added shuffling past hastily.

As his father shut him out of the bathroom, Alex returned to his new room to decide the best course of action for the rest of the day. Greeted by the mirror as he re-entered the room, Alex looked at his reflection. It felt as though he was seeing an old friend for the first time in years. The colour had started to return to his cheeks, his freshly shaved face glistened as his dark green eyes started to regain a flicker of happiness. His attention was drawn to his scrawny, undernourished body. It was a far cry from the finely tuned body image he had wanted to attain before his life became so complicated.

Getting dressed, he made a mental note of his tasks for the day. In the past weeks, he used to have a tick list of tasks to do before he let himself be dragged into the abyss of his imagination. However, today he no longer needed that list. He vowed that he would be in control today.

Drying his hair, he flung some clothes on and left the house with his sizable winter coat. During the rest of the day he managed to get his hair cut back into its old shape and meet with his course tutor at the university. Throughout his troubled relationship he'd been juggling his private life with a course in criminology. His studies had suffered through the unpredictability of his life at that time. But now he wanted to remedy his mistake and get his life back on track.

His course tutor considered the picture Alex presented to him.

"This is a very interesting situation. Have you any evidence to substantiate your appeal for extenuating circumstances."

Alex took a second to think before reaching into one of his pockets. The lecturer's nose crinkled in contempt; Rockshore University never had a shortage of students looking for extra time. Retrieving a small box from his pocket, Alex placed it on the table, along with a piece of paper, and slid them to his lecturer.

Confused, the lecturer investigated, his face dropping as he found it was a doctor's prescription for heart medication. Alex waited, scratching the back of his neck which still itched after his hair cut prior to the meeting. Noticing the horror on the lecturer's face, he added:

"I've been through a lot these past few months, stress affects blood pressure, which affects the body, and if the body isn't functioning right the chances are the mind won't be doing too good either."

Realising the severity of Alex's situation, his tutor

encouraged him to put his appeal in writing and offered to support him in any way he could.

Satisfied with what he had accomplished with his afternoon, Alex made his way back home to begin paving his road to academic redemption. By the end of the day, he had not only completed his appeal but he had also made a start on his coursework. As the night progressed, he felt a sudden urge to leave the house. After imprisoning himself in a dark, oxygen-deprived tip for a month, he had developed a sense of cabin fever. At first he wanted to go to the public library; however, the memories of meeting Angelica there made him reluctant to do so. Instead he decided to visit the university library.

Making his way to his new destination, Alex vowed to continue his studies. He felt a certain sense of productivity in his journey to the library, his music blasting in his ears as the cold night air brushed his shaved sensitive face, and his winter jacket blowing in the wind.

However, once he arrived at the library the momentum he had picked up and utilised during the day was starting to fade. Arriving at the library, Alex turned off his old music player, wrapping the earphones around it as he observed his new surroundings.

The entrance to the library was a social courtyard; there were groups of people sat around in study groups. Alex felt his serotonin levels start to drop as he looked around the groups of people at the tables. He sensed an overbearing air of falseness in the atmosphere.

Most of the students weren't studying, they were just socializing. However, to Alex none of them seemed genuinely happy. They either appeared insecure and awkward or arrogant and over-confident.

A couple of minutes passed and a nearby vending machine caught Alex's eye. He thought to himself that his sugar levels were probably low. He bought a sugary beverage for the road and turned to leave.

All of a sudden, a numbing sensation spread across his

chest as his heart raced, his body was once again filled with adrenaline. He caught a glimpse of Angelica outside the library in amongst the usual crowd of loitering students. Naturally, she stood out in the crowd to Alex. Her black leather trench coat blew in the wind, showing off her expensive red dress shirt, dark trousers and boots, an outfit Alex had seen her in many times before.

In a moment of realisation, it became apparent she was heading towards the library. Unfortunately for Alex, the entrance was also the only way out. Trying to avoid crossing paths with his estranged love, Alex hurried up a side stair case within the library. Worried she might be going up as well, he went to the very top floor.

There was a darkened balcony up there which had been closed off to the public, a large potted plant blocking access to it. In a rushed effort, Alex squeezed his wiry frame past the giant plant. Feeling the effects of his racing heartbeat, Alex sat on the windowsill of the balcony. Feeling the sweat cascading off his brow, he scrambled to collect his thoughts in spite of his visible panic.

Down in the open forecourt, 35 feet below where Alex was sitting, Angelica sat down at a table on her own. She placed her reading glasses on her face and proceeded to read her book, peering over the volume and scanning the room. Angelica would regularly go to places on her own for meals and various other activities.

In an effort to console himself, Alex had cracked open his canned fizzy drink. If nothing else, the shot of sugar was good for shock, regardless of what the health experts said. He felt trapped and awkward. He didn't want to confront her as he knew she was capable of causing chaos even without meaning to. Eventually he started to calm down as his body adapted to the excess adrenaline. Alex started to realise the anonymous and strategic advantage his position offered.

He could see everyone but, because of his secluded, restricted and elevated location, they couldn't see him.

It felt as though he had an opportunity to see what her life was like without him. The tension had settled slightly in his stomach and in his chest; however, he felt an ongoing sense of anxiety dawn over his soul. In a sense, it felt as though he was stalking her, despite the fact he was trapped and unable to move due to his feeling of unease. Alex diverted his attentions from her, observing the whole forecourt and everyone in it.

Alex's anxiety diminished; he started to take comfort in being able to see everyone in the room. The height of his position and the viewpoint empowered Alex at a time when he felt his weakest. As the minutes went by, he found himself questioning things: angst about his university course, what he would do after university, and if it was worth even fighting to stay there. His mind was running negative loops; however, his soul still felt at peace overlooking the gathering of students below him.

Suddenly, Angelica closed her book and grabbed her bag, running out of the building in tears. The randomness of the outburst drew Alex's mind back to her. He wondered whether to go after her. While he sat there working through his dilemma, Alex noticed a young man enter the library. He had similar hair to Alex and bore a strong resemblance to him from afar. Visibly startled, the young man turned to see why Angelica was running away.

The chain of events had created a scene and attracted the attention of the rest of the people in the forecourt. A male onlooker approached the young man, enquiring in a cockney accent:

"Oi mate. What did you do to her? She looked terrified!"

The confused young man claimed he'd never seen her before in his life and had no idea why she reacted like that. Alex started to realise that Angelica had thought the young man was him.

However, he had never expected such a dramatic reaction. The way she had fled the building in tears like that would naturally make people assume the worst about whoever she was running from.

It wasn't a surprise to Alex as he had seen her create some chaotic nightmares during their relationship, sometimes without even realising it. He felt the breathtaking sensation of fear coursing through his chest once more. Knowing she was out of the building, Alex started to make his way downstairs, out of the building and back home.

Arriving back at the house, he returned to his room to try and finish his coursework. Refreshed by the cleanliness his room provided, he managed to convert his fear into motivation to succeed, manipulating his own emotions to complete his coursework. He lost himself in his work, managing to focus entirely on getting the task in hand completed.

It came to midnight by the time he had finished his work. Alex was faced with a choice, one he faced on a regular basis. He could either go to bed, getting ready for another day, or he could stay up a while, have some fizzy drinks and see what he could do with the rest of the night. Just as in the past Alex was faced with this dilemma and, similar to most students, he chose to stay up.

This would prove to be a bad move, as he resorted to the internet for entertainment. He found himself on a social media site called Open-Options. His intentions started off productively as he wanted to cultivate new friendships to help him to move on to a happier chapter in his life.

Unfortunately for Alex though, thoughts of Angelica came rushing back into his mind. His imagination slowly stirred. The darkness of the night brought Alex's creative thinking to life, still in deep mourning over his lost love and trying to comprehend the loneliness his soul felt.

Unaware of the cognitive crisis he was about to endure, Alex continued to look up old friends and social groups at the university. Each click drew him closer to stumbling across something which would remind him of her.

Sitting in his comfortable chair, he had set off on a path to subconscious self-destruction. By the end of the night he had managed to convince himself that none of the productivity he had accomplished that day mattered and that fate was against him. At around three o'clock he gave up, retiring to his cold, clean bed, yearning for the imaginary friend he had fallen in love with.

9 o'clock in the morning came; Derick's bed creaked as he dragged his lethargic body upright. He staggered up the corridor, his eyes looking down at the worn beige carpet below his feet. Once he had finished in the bathroom and was fully awake, he returned down the corridor.

He poked his head round the corner of his son's room. Looking in at him, he saw a small collection of cans surrounding Alex's computer. Derick looked at Alex who was still fast asleep in bed, his bedside cabinet covered in tear-soaked tissues.

"How the mighty have fallen. Still, there'll be fight in the old boy yet,"

Derick mocked as he pulled the door too and left his son to sleep in his bed of sorrow.

He made his way downstairs and continued writing his book. Being a former doorman, Derick maintained a dry sense of humour and a gruff exterior. He wanted to help his son; alas, after years of containing his own emotions, he didn't know how.

At around 2 o'clock in the afternoon, Alex woke up with a start. He felt numb once again, caught in an internal struggle of wanting Angelica back and accepting it was impossible.

He had still made progress as opposed to where he had been a couple of days earlier, but he found himself in a never-ending cycle. Feeling less energised than he did the day before, the depression had taken its toll. Alex lay exhausted, trying to motivate himself to get out of bed. He had achieved everything he wanted to the day before and yet he didn't feel like he had progressed.

Caught up in his despair, Alex didn't realise his bedroom door was slowly opening. Derick's large Celtic head squeezed through the gap:

"Oh Alex… Are you looking for a reason to get out of bed? How about you get your lazy arse out of the house and find a job so you can pay me some rent."

His father's softly spoken sarcasm prompted Alex to get up. He was irritated by his father's disdain for his feelings, but didn't have the energy to argue. After realising gaining work experience wasn't a bad idea, he heeded Derick's words, got dressed and printed off a C.V. setting off in search of a job.

Happy to get out of the house, Alex found an advertisement for a position at a hardware store on the university jobs board. Not wasting any time, he phoned the shop and managed to gain an interview that very day. He hadn't had much luck with gaining employment prior to his university course; however, the title of student meant that he wasn't over qualified for the position, and the fact he was at university and had a good attendance record showed he was reliable.

To his pleasant surprise, the store manager Arthur Harding instantly warmed to him. Perhaps the most defining factor was that he was subconsciously pre-occupied, which alleviated the pressure of nerves. After a successful interview he decided to go for a long walk. He knew it was only a temporary distraction from his woes, but the fresh air and freedom seemed much more appealing than being cooped up at home.

The overcast day showed glimmers of prosperity as sunshine peeped through the muggy grey clouds. Reaching the town centre, Alex ventured into the town square. At night the town square was crawling with drunkards and party-going students. However, during the day it reflected a different side of society with a much more varied group of people. He admired the architecture of the town hall. A large stoic building that had endured years of English history, from its opening in the 1800's before Rockshore had turned from a town to a city, to the present day.

Having moved down to stay with his father from elsewhere, he hadn't taken the time to properly appreciate his surroundings. Not only did he appreciate the historical architecture before his eyes, but he also started to relate to it. In an effort to try and comprehend the apprehension and guilt his mind continuously resonated with, Alex found himself constantly relating aspects of the outside world to his inner conflicts.

Eager to digest his revelation, Alex sat down on a nearby bench. Retrieving a pen and an old note pad he had left in his pocket, he started to sketch the architectural spectacle. The sunlight which had pierced through the overcast clouds beamed down on the page, beckoning his creative expression to flow. Though it was only a rough drawing, the creative expression helped him to alleviate his pain.

Suddenly his creative endeavour was halted by a deafening shriek. Startled, Alex's eyes rolled off the page to identify the source. To his disbelief, he saw, down a nearby side street, a sinister hooded hoodlum, trying to wrestle a purse from a girl.

He felt a deep anger emerging from within his stomach. Adrenaline coursing through his body, Alex heroically rose from the bench and ran towards the crime in progress. Sprinting as fast as he could, he approached the side street. To his frustration, by the time he reached them, the thief had commandeered the purse and was getting away.

Alex gave chase, pursuing the hooded figure down an alley and onto another main street.

Noble as his intentions were, Alex's poor dietary choices and lack of physical conditioning had caught up with him. He could feel his body slowing as his heart raced on.

Hyperventilating and out of breath, Alex stopped,

clasping his chest.

The thief had escaped.

Adding insult to injury, a boorish passer-by laughed:

"Really? What were you going to do if you caught him? Go and get a burger, you scrawny twat."

Out of breath and embarrassed, Alex made his way back to the south side of town.

Despite his earlier success in gaining employment, Alex felt utterly helpless, vulnerable and humiliated. A little later, the humbled would-be hero returned home. Derick was eager to hear how his son's job hunt had gone and was impressed with Alex's efforts.

He appreciated how difficult it was to gain employment in the economic climate of the day.

"So you managed to get an interview today, you like the manager and it sounds like you've done well in the interview; so why are you no' smiling?"

Derick enquired in his gruff Scottish manner.

Though his body had recovered from his burst of exercise, Alex's soul was still in a lot of pain. The concentrated dose of embarrassment he had felt earlier, paired with his underlying feelings of grief bubbled away under his unfulfilled demeanour. He knew he may regret it but, Alex decided to confide in his father about what had happened, and his frustrations at not being able to rescue the unknown victim from her unknown attacker. Hearing his son's burdens, Derick sat in reflection.

It was difficult to read his expressions when he was listening intently. Derick had developed his poker face during his time as a doorman. He now had a better understanding of ways to help his son and had formulated a plan in his head. Derick kept the majority of his thoughts to himself; however, after a slight pause, he responded:

"When did you turn into Mr Jolly Big Bollocks?"

Alex felt a rush of anger flowing back into his Celtic blood. Infuriated by his father's cavalier attitude he erupted:

"I've had it! All you do is sleep, watch T.V., pretend to write and take the piss out of me.

Angelica and I had planned a future together. We were going travel the world together! She'd travelled around the world before she met me; the furthest I've got from my home town is this hell hole! She used to say British people had no soul. Now I think she's right.

I shouldn't have left her, she was my one true love and I ruined it because she didn't fit into a country I now hate!"

Derick sat back and listened to his son's heartfelt roar of pain and regret. He had goaded him into ranting so he could empathise with him. Once Alex had said his piece, Derick responded in a calmer tone which Alex hadn't heard before, doing his best to keep the peace:

"Alex Douglas, before this conversation, you and I were virtual strangers. We hadn't seen each other in years and you moved down here out of convenience to go to university.

You've lived here for a year, the latter part of which, you spent all of your time with Angelica.

You're an introvert young man; you've isolated yourself from near enough all social aspects of university. That's half the reason these smart-arsed buggers go in the first place, so they can have a good time.

You spent all of your time with one person, things didn't work out and now you've been dragged out of your comfort zone and you haven't got anyone to pick up the pieces for you, except for some bloody shrink."

Alex started to hear his father's words of wisdom for the first time. He then realised that out of the ashes of his meltdown he had the opportunity to develop healthier relationships, relationships with people better suited to his personality.

Noticing his son's unspoken receptiveness, Derick

continued:

"If you truly want to go back to her then do it, but you'll soon see why you needed to escape in the first place. I for one don't want you to, for fear of your personal safety.

She made mincemeat out of you before you dropped her.

Hell hath no fury like a woman's scorned, far less that delusional ding-bat.

From an outside perspective though, there's no good or bad people in bad relationships and break-ups, there's just two people trying to come to terms with the pain they feel. Hell, the vast majority of fights I dealt with on the door all those years ago were caused by the irrationalities of love and loss. You may feel guilty, but you needn't. You were only doing your best and in her own way I'm sure she was too."

Consoled by the seasoned knowledge his father had bestowed upon him, Alex's temper was pacified. He appreciated his father's words and thanked him before he went back upstairs to reflect. As he left, Derick called after him:

"And believe me, you're not the only one in this family who can't run!"

Later that evening, Alex once again felt trapped within the house. Despite it being close to 10 o'clock, he ventured out to explore the city's nightlife. This would be the first time he had embarked on such an endeavour since his break up.

Derick could hear Alex getting ready to go out from his sofa. Looking at the clock in astonishment at the time, he put down his notes:

"Where are you going at this time of night?"
he asked with concern.
Alex explained he wanted to go out and clear his head.

Hoping there was a hidden ambition to move on, Derick replied:

"Good for you, before you go though, go up to my room and take one of those Wa-hey-tex condoms out of the bottom drawer. They're underneath the dirty mags. On the off chance you pick up another crazy, you'll no be getting her up the duff."

Irritated by his father's narrow-mindedness, Alex bid his father goodnight and left the house, wearing his signature baggy, pocketed jacket.

Derick sighed to himself in apprehension:

"I hope he's gonna be alright. Maybe I should give my old friend a call. He'll no be ready for these streets at this time of night."

With the ambition of exploring a different part of the town, Alex set off for Ravens-dale Road. Ravens-dale Road was a very popular location for night life.

It offered a variety of pubs, clubs and multi-cultural restaurants (many of which were open all night) making it a popular location for pub-crawling.

It was the exact type of place Alex would normally avoid as he did not drink alcohol. However, something was drawing him to it this evening. He hadn't gone out with the intention of making friends or meeting new people, he just wanted to scout the town and see a different style of life.

Arriving at the end of the road, it became clear he was about to embark on something of an urban safari.

Uncouth noises echoed around the vicinity, accompanied by vulgar sights of lust, rage and rambunctiousness: reflecting the stereotypical behaviour he wanted to avoid.

As he continued, an amalgamation of booming music and overbearing voices could be heard, seasoned with foul language and a vast range of amplified emotions. Alex's sober senses were overloaded by the primitive environment ahead of him. Despite being far from his comfort zone, something was willing Alex on through this spontaneous and seemingly pointless journey.

Further progressing down the street, his nose was assaulted with a range of strong aromas. The smell of alcohol and cigarette smoke filled the crowded street. Alex found his sinuses being attacked by the strong scent of aftershave and deodorants that passers-by had clarted themselves in.

Even though the street courted so much chaos, the darkness of the night contrasted with the various lighting which illuminated the street made for a visually impressive sight. Each of the pubs and clubs was occupied by doormen wearing orange high-visibility jackets, stationed to curtail the commotion within their respective turfs.

Suddenly Alex's attention was drawn away from the view.

He quickly stepped back as a heavily inebriated woman vomited in the middle of the pavement.

"Your missus is an animal mate,"

a disgruntled spectator snarled at the man next to her.

The agitated man assisting her angrily replied:

"You what mate?"

Defending his companion's dignity, he squared up to their antagonist, inadvertently allowing his companion to fall face first into a pool of her own puke. Before further conversation was attempted they were in a drunken brawl.

Alex carried on down the road, avoiding the conflict while passers-by cheered and a couple of doormen moved in to separated and restrain the two combatants.

Having witnessed enough social atrocities the alcohol-fuelled environment was creating, Alex turned down a side road. Having never drunk before, he found himself questioning what was so enjoyable about being in the situation he'd just witnessed. Once he had created distance between himself and the overbearing noises of Ravens-dale road, Alex's senses started to quieten.

The streets were largely home to student accommodation and residential housing. A few moments into the quiet, strange noises could be heard coming from a nearby side street. Curious to see what was going on, Alex's senses heightened with anxiety as he peered round the corner. It was a group of what appeared to be students. They were staggering up the residential side street in a drunk and disorderly fashion, singing at the top of their voices.

Their mortifying medley caused an outraged old man to call out to them from his bedroom window:

"Will you idiots shut up, it's almost midnight and I'm trying to sleep!"

The students had stopped to face the man; behind them was a local repair garage with a forecourt surrounded by a brick wall. Three out of the four students looked embarrassed by and apologetic for their actions. However, one of the students seemed irritated that their song had been interrupted.

Placing the bottle of plonk he'd been carrying on the side of the wall behind him, the disgruntled young man started to argue.

"What's the problem? We're not even being that loud,"

he shouted as he staggered back into the wall.

About to make another point, the excitably sloshed young man flailed his arms in the air, knocking the bottle off the wall.

The bottle smashed on impact with the concrete carpark, followed by a blood curdling scream.

Startled by the chain of events, the students fled the area, while the old man moaned:

"Wonderful, they've woken the neighbourhood tramp. Now I'll never get to sleep,"

slamming his double glazed window shut.

Appalled by the apathy he'd witnessed, Alex rushed to the carpark to investigate the damage. He reached the area as the screams continued. The visibility behind the wall was very limited due to the poorly lit street. Alex peered around the corner at the injured silhouette lying under the shadow of the wall.

Alex was anxious to help; however, the poorly lit conditions of the area presented a hazard, and he didn't want to stand on the victim. Alex wished he had a torch on him.

It was difficult to think with the suddenness of the situation; however, Alex came to his senses and used the glow of his old phone to gain a clearer picture. He could see the shattered glass and a horrifying combination of blood and wine on the floor. Lying against the wall was a wounded tramp with scraggy long grey hair and dirty combat gear. His face was twisted in pain as he had a shard of glass embedded in the area around his eye. The blood trickled down to his unkempt beard.

"Are you alright sir?"

Alex asked nervously.

The tramp's screams quietened as he sat up to see who he was talking to.

"That must be the first time someone's called me sir in over 20 years."

The tramp commented in surprise, still exhaling in pain.

"I'll call an ambulance for you."

Alex exclaimed readying his phone.

"Don't be daft son, I appreciate the gesture but the ambulances will be busy enough on a Friday night, they ain't gonna come down here to pick me up for a cut like this. I've taken much worse in my time."

Realising the naivety of his offer, Alex said he'd pay for a taxi to take him to hospital.

Somewhat touched by the kindness of the random stranger stood before him, the tramp smiled.

His conceptions of the country's youth had been positively changed within a few moments of Alex's company.

Once Alex had finished organising the taxi, the tramp introduced himself

"Charles Cartwright, what's your name young man?"

Alex introduced himself, shaking the former war hero's hand. There was a delay for the taxi service due to the increase of trade they received on a Friday night. Charles and Alex took the opportunity to get to know each other better.

Naturally, their conversation quickly turned to Alex's ex and how he struggled to deal with day-to-day life following the loss of his love. Despite being an old school military man, Charles empathised with Alex's situation. He gave Alex a valuable piece of advice which would help him combat his conflicting internal conundrum:

"You'll only see what you want to, until you see what you have to."

With the words of wisdom bestowed upon him by his newly found ally, he was able to put Angelica to one side for a short period of time. Charles's hindsight had momentarily defused the myth Alex had created in his mind.

It wasn't long before the taxi arrived and took the two unlikely friends to the hospital. By the time Alex got home it was around 4 o'clock in the morning.

Charles was content being dropped at the edge of the city as he didn't have an address to go to. Despite the feeling of physical tiredness and fatigue, Alex could feel a genuine sense of satisfaction resonating within his soul.

He had helped someone in a situation where everyone else had done nothing. Consequently, his good deeds allowed him a period of peace. Retiring to his bed, he drifted off to sleep feeling that he had made the most of the night and earned his rest.

While Alex enjoyed his well-earned slumber, his father was relieved to see his son was home safely. Although he was relieved, he didn't want his son's safety to be compromised by the night life in the future. With this in mind, Derick took the liberty of contacting his old friend, Nick Norman; a retired police man, who taught martial arts at a community centre in the outskirts of the city. Nick was delighted to hear from Derick after such a long time and understood Derick's concerns about his son's safety venturing out at night.

Alex had a reasonably quiet week, filled with junk food and T.V.; naturally his emotions fluctuated throughout the week. However, he had advanced to a more normal reaction to his father's bullish banter. The following week, Alex attended his first class with Nick. Due to his experience as a police officer and his passion for martial arts, Nick had tailored his classes to incorporate martial arts with self-defence scenarios. Additionally, his legal acumen and sharpened street smarts enabled him to develop a program which taught his students an urbanised version of the skill.

Following his first lesson, Nick pulled Alex to one side and made an effort to get to know his new student. Alex started to get a sense of Nick's in-depth knowledge through his appearance. His face reflected the eclectic experiences he'd encountered during his life, his pale cheeks highlighted with hints of pink.

Nick's face reflected the wisdom he had accumulated through the various trials and tribulations he had experienced; his short silver hair had been bleached by different climates on various journeys around the world. His most distinctive feature, his educated pale blue eyes looked into Alex's soul, as they had done with so many others around the world.

Alex explained he'd been at a loss lately owing to his break up and that he couldn't turn to alcohol as he didn't drink. He felt a sense of embarrassment about disclosing this, as he knew Nick and his father had been to many pubs together.

Sensing his insecurity, his new Sensei reassured him:

"The courts, prison cells, hospitals and even cemeteries are filled with people who have to deal with the consequences of uncontrolled drunken decisions. Alcohol creates jobs but it also creates problems, avoiding them is nothing to be ashamed of.

As far as heartbreak goes, you won't be the same again but, if you survive the transition, you can emerge from the ashes, like a phoenix: brighter, bolder and with the freedom to get wherever you want to in life. You're always welcome to train here with me. The energy and range of emotions you feel right now can all be channelled into positive, healthy exercise to increase your quality of life."

Alex not only felt grateful that he had found an insightful mentor, but he also allowed himself to realise that he wasn't alone in how he felt. He came to realise that there were a lot of opportunities and knowledge to be discovered in life. Through this traumatic period, Alex felt an uncontrollable desire to help people. However, he realised his own physical limitations.

He asked Nick if there was anything he could do to maintain his safety in case he needed to defend himself before he was physically ready.

Nick sensed that there may have been an ulterior motive to Alex's question, but he didn't want to send one of his students out unprepared when they had asked for help.

Although Nick had been out of the police game for several years, he was still passionate about keeping people safe, especially his students.

Nick invited Alex to wait with him till the others had gone. Once they were alone, he took Alex over to his duffel bag filled with what appeared to be random items. He picked up a paper with the headlines reading "The Sea Side Saxons"

Alex's mind started to wonder as Nick rolled up the newspaper "What on earth are the Sea Side Saxon's…"

Suddenly, Alex was hunched over in shock with a short, sharp pain in his stomach.

"Well for starters you need to pay attention at all times Alex!"

Nick reminded his inexperienced student. Alex looked up to discover Nick had rolled the newspaper up so tightly it had become a legalised weapon. Now Nick undoubtedly had Alex's attention, he addressed his confused student:

"If you carry a weapon you'll be arrested or potentially worse. An enemy won't expect a newspaper to be a threat and a police officer won't arrest you if you defend yourself with a legal object you were carrying for another purpose. But obviously I'd advise against going out looking for trouble."

Alex respectfully heeded his new mentor's warning and agreed to see him at the next lesson, thanking him for his additional advice.

Following the lesson, Alex received more good news; he discovered he had a voicemail message from the store manager Arthur Harding informing him when he would be starting his position of employment at the Cutting Craft hardware store.

Feeling satisfied with his achievements, Alex returned home to rest his freshly trained body. He knew his emotions would sometimes get the better of him and still haunt him. However, he felt a sense of pride in the person he had the capacity to become, through the opportunities he could pursue in his unwritten future.

Within a couple of days Alex started his new part time job. His new work place, Cutting Craft, was a spacious hardware shop located in one of the more upmarket shopping districts of the city.

It was rather an old-fashioned shop which hadn't been refurbished since the '80s. The shop had a great sense of history to it and reminded Alex of the small village he came from across the country. Freshly employed, Alex was very happy at his new place of work and eager to expand his knowledge and performance in the retail industry. His manager was a kind old man who appreciated Alex's efforts.

Alex was keen to learn from and impress his manager as he appreciated he was somewhat of a retail veteran with years of experience behind him. Arthur was happy to teach his new employee everything he knew. Alex's co-workers were friendly people as well; however, Alex hadn't much of a chance to see all of them as a result of their varying shifts and his limited hours of work.

Outside of his new work environment, Alex spent his time putting the frantic finishing touches to his Criminology assignments and training with Nick, unleashing the energy his stress had built up while enhancing his fitness and educating his reflexes.

When he wasn't focused on studying, training or working, he felt an unnervingly, crippling sense of aimlessness. He had trained himself to focus on anything that could take his attention away from the demon lurking in the depths of his mind.

He even felt moments where he enjoyed life. Sadly, underneath, he knew nothing compared to the spiritually intimate connection Alex felt between himself and the forbidden fruit of his first love. Nonetheless, Alex carried on.

It wasn't long before Alex's weeks began to take on a steady structure. It turned to be a cycle of work, studying and training. As a result of this, he found that his mind, body, work experience and bank account were expanding through each of these positive activities.

Furthermore, Alex had managed to supress his feelings through this cycle, constantly keeping himself stimulated, either physically or mentally. The martial arts training Alex received from Nick allowed him to combine his body and his mind. At the same time, Alex valued his time under Arthur's seasoned tutelage at Cutting Craft, developing his skills in customer service.

When he wasn't at work, Alex would go for runs, study or lift weights in his room (which had been turned into a glorified gym/office).

Before Alex knew it, it was May. Much like the greenery of the season, Alex's life was blossoming into a new chapter. He didn't give himself a chance to let his mind stray from these activities. He just took each day as it came and told himself that he was working towards the future.

As far as his father was concerned, Alex was back on track. He had a part time job, he was making progress towards his degree, he was physically fit and he fitted every criteria of a decent member of society. In light of his son's accomplishments, his father refrained from encouraging Alex to socialise. Although Derrick was delighted with his son's progress, deep down, he sensed that an ill-timed comment could throw his routine out of sync.

Being involved in ordinary social occasions and situations bored Alex. He wanted to do something more meaningful.

Below the surface of Alex's soul, there was a deep desire to rescue people. When the troubled young man wasn't occupied with a specific task, he would often wander around various parts of the town, desperately seeking a meaningful purpose to distract himself from the underlying emptiness he felt.

Despite his setbacks during the year, Alex achieved impressive grades, and managed to progress to the next year of his degree. Derick was extremely proud of his son for how much he had achieved within such a short period of time. However, he couldn't help but notice that Alex still didn't feel as relaxed and accomplished as he should. What Derick didn't know however, was the more Alex had achieved the more he was running out of distractions from his unresolved feelings.

As spring came to its adolescence, a notable change occurred, a sizable shift which threw a monkey wrench into Alex's perfect routine. Cutting Craft was purchased by a larger chain of shops, Arthur Harding retired and a new manager took over the store.

Arthur had become an irreplaceable figure in Alex's life; his replacement, Bill McCray, would become the bane of Alex's existence. Bill had gained the managerial position partly through his experience in management, but mostly through political angling with the company who had purchased the store. Whereas Arthur had managed the shop with a genuine love for his community and providing a service, Bill was used to utilizing underhand tactics to meet targets and save as much money as he could.

Bill's egomaniacal and controlling attitude quickly alienated the other staff members. Some members of staff began to leave and, in their place, Bill employed likeminded people to work for him. Within a few weeks of working with Bill and his new cohorts, Alex started to notice the negative impact the new regime was having on the work place and the team morale.

Arthur had always encouraged Alex to speak his mind, reassuring him that his opinions could make a difference. Unfortunately, Alex made the mistake of airing his observations to Bill. Outraged, Bill started to resent Alex from that moment on.

Alex was required to sign a new work contract with the company which had taken over the shop.

To his unpleasant surprise, he discovered that Bill had reduced his hours on his new contract. He couldn't prove it, but he knew that it was a result of his comments to him the week before.

With his hours reduced and his workplace infested with negativity, Alex found his structured work toward the future spiralling out of control. He didn't want to be pushed out of the job he'd put so much into, but the influx of negativity made it difficult to ignore the void of unhappiness in his life.

As the weeks went on, Derick began to find the atmosphere building in the house once again, with his sulking son becoming unbearable. One fateful night, the house was hot as the tensions began to rise between father and son. Alex sat on an armchair in the corner of the living room adjacent to Derick. The radio was on in the background while Derick was trying to write, but he was unable to concentrate through the vibes of misery emanating from Alex's aura.

Finally breaking the deafening silence, Derick snapped, shutting his note book:

"Right I've had it; you've achieved everything you're in this town to do. You've got a job, you're fit as a fiddle and you're back on track for your university course. Not to mention, compared to most students, your bank account's thriving; but you're sat here skulking in the corner of the room like the grim bloody reaper."

Derick's rant was interrupted by an emergency news broadcast over the local radio station.

The broadcast warned of a riot at the Town Cryer pub. To Derick's horror he saw Alex's eyes light up with inspired purpose.

Alex sprang from his arm chair. Despite the fact he had never been near a fight since school, he knew that there would be people in danger down there. Following his months of combat and fitness training, Alex felt confident he would be competent enough to make a difference.

"Now hold on a minute and don't be so stupid!"

Derick exclaimed, turning on the T.V. to their local news channel to discourage his son from entering the fray.

By that point, Alex was out of his seat and lunging for the door. Sprinting out of the house and down the street, Alex felt a fire and energy he had never felt before. He finally felt he might be able to make as much of a difference to someone's life as he once had done to Angelica's.

He started to realise that being in such an intense relationship with someone like that was similar to being in the secret service. Nothing compared to it, and it was impossible for the average person to comprehend its intensity. He'd never felt as alive, the rush of unknown risk and prosperity flowed through him as he ran towards the town centre.

Alex slowed his pace to conserve energy as he approached the scene of the riot. As he drew closer, the darkness of night having enveloped the summer's evening, it occurred to him that he may have ventured too far out of his depth. He could hear the raised voices and smashing of glass as he approached the area. Peering round a corner, Alex could see the riot from afar.

The police had created a cordon; however, they were grossly outnumbered by the rioters and could only create barriers to contain the chaos. Alex took an obscure detour down the back alleys leading to the town square where the riot was most centred.

The sight of all the violence and chaos made Alex wish he'd brought some improvised weapons with him. However, he doubted the effectiveness of a newspaper in a situation this volatile. Though his body was riddled with fear, the adrenaline and danger invigorated his soul. He finally had the opportunity to rise to the occasion and make a difference.

On his way down a cobbled alley, he came across a young man lying prone on the ground with a hooded figure stood above him holding a knife.

Wasting no time, Alex quickly crept up on the hooded assailant and pushed him head first into the wall. The impact of the thug's head hitting the wall disorientated him enough for Alex to disarm him. Once Alex had confiscated the knife, the thug ran off towards the town square. Having cleared the secluded alley of danger, Alex attended to the victim of the attempted murder.

Although he had not yet been seriously injured, the young man was clearly shaken by the event and unable to communicate properly. Alex reached into his pocket and gave the young man £20 to get a taxi home. He told him to follow the alley back where Alex had come from. The young man felt a debt of gratitude to Alex and introduced himself as Osgood, scribbling his mobile number on a piece of paper from his pocket. Taking Osgood's number, Alex made his way back to the riot to see if there were any other people he could help.

By that time, the police were starting to regain control of the situation, as reinforcements had shown up. Alex walked into the town square in front of the Town Cryer pub, scanning the area for potential victims. The various brawls around the area were slowly coming to an end as the police established their presence. While the flames of chaos were being extinguished, Alex observed the broken windows, smashed glass and bodies lying motionless on the pavement. His eyes scanned the area trying to comprehend the chaos as he cautiously approached the scene.

He heard a female scream from down an alley behind the pub.

Something sounded familiar about the voice. Suddenly his concentration was disrupted as a glass bottle smashed against the pub wall half a foot from his face. Keeping his head down, Alex sprinted toward the source of the scream, avoiding detection from both the police and the rioters.

As he turned the corner, he made his way down the shadowy alley.

At the end of the alley there was a small clearing which was lit by a street light. Alex noticed a figure moving in front of him in the shadows. Staying out of sight, he continued to watch.

An eerily familiar voice shouted from the clearing:
"No, stay away! You should not approach me."

Alex's eyes widened in disbelief as he recognised Angelica's distinctive European accent. His heart beat faster and faster and his chest became tight. The silhouette in the shadows continued to approach Angelica. Alex's adrenaline relocated from his heart to his mind and he made his move to save her from the unknown threat that lurked before him.

Grasping the approaching figure by the arm, he turned him around and delivered a swift knee to the sternum. The blow drove the air out of the man as he fell to the floor winded, landing in what sounded like a pile of rubbish bags.

Satisfied the unkempt unknown assailant had been dealt with, Alex's attention turned back to the clearing where the estranged love of his life stood petrified in the warm glow of the street light above her.

Angelica's pale complexion was illuminated as her eyes glistened with apprehension. Alex cautiously made his way toward the clearing, preparing to reveal himself. Angelica's dyed black and sapphire hair looked more vibrant in person than he had remembered.

There she stood before him, in living colour, wearing the long dark wavy skirt he had bought for her birthday, with a black leather corset and silky black cardigan. Alex approached, taking in the gothic and dangerous beauty before his eyes.

He asked:

"Are you alright Angelica? I'm sorry things didn't work out between us. But you're safe now."

After a brief pause of shock, Angelica's vulnerable eyes met Alex's for the first time in what felt like forever. All of a sudden the fear in her eyes evaporated and turned to uncontainable fury, which burst out into her screeching response

"No! I'm not ok. I hate this filthy country and all of the soulless people who live here. This place is toxic, and you! You broke my heart! Even though I gave you everything,

YOU BROKE MY HEART!"

Alex stuttered, trying to defend himself. His attempt was interrupted by a swift slap to his confused face. Tears of fury filled her fiery eyes, exposing the true demon he had feared facing for so long.

The pain of the slap and the harpy-like scream which Alex suffered, shattered his illusions of the imaginary friend his guilt ridden subconscious had concocted.

"Evening all, what's going on down here then?"

A couple of police officers enquired as they investigated the alley. Flabbergasted by the chain of events, Alex stood stunned.

Angelica cried out:

"He was going to try and rape me and kill me."

The blood drained from Alex's face as he remembered that he had heard her falsely accuse others of sexual assaults during their storied and troubled relationship.

Now he found himself on the receiving end of her slanderous accusations. In front of two officers of the law no less.

The police officers approached sternly looking to question their suspect of his actions.

"HAHAHA, oh Alex my boy you really did pick a nut job there, son. She's talking tripe officers. I tried to help her to safety but she screamed, so the lad took me down and got a right rollicking from her. He's a good lad officers'. God awful taste in women though, bloody hell, sort it out lad."

To Alex's astonishment, the man he had incapacitated was none other than his acquaintance Charles. Mortified that he had attacked him and very thankful that he defended him in front of the police, Alex apologised profusely. Somewhat bemused at the situation, the officers turned to Angelica for a further explanation.

"Aren't you going to arrest them? Ugh! I've had it with this country; your British police are so corrupt!"

Angelica snarled.

The police started to realise the delusional accusations and told all parties to disperse from the area.

Charles laughed:

"Oh damn, I was getting quite comfortable on this here pile of bags."

The jolly tramp arose from his pile of rubbish and left the alley with Alex who was trying to comprehend the chain of events that had occurred through night. He was thankful that Charles was there to save him from the potential consequences of Angelica's delusional accusations.

Grateful he had evaded physical or legal harm in such a chaotic and reckless environment, Alex and Charles left the alley, abandoning the unbalanced and troubled young lady, along with all the illusions of guilt his heart had burdened him with.

They walked the quietened streets in a comfortable silence as the police had quickly regained control. However, a particular sight amongst the clearing chaos caught Alex's eye. A group of paramedics crowded around a motionless body on the floor. They were desperately trying to resuscitate the young man, who was around his age. He had been stabbed and had an oxygen mask over his face as he was carried into an ambulance in a stretcher.

It was at that moment, Alex realised the sheer inadequacy of his self-loathing and heartbreak in comparison to someone so young, fighting for his life.

The image perfectly represented how fragile mortal life was. An image so powerful and so close to Alex, he began to cherish how precious his life was. In seconds he was swiftly awoken to the potential opportunities he had.

He heard the vibration of his phone in his jacket pocket. Alex took out his phone and saw a text from the young man he had saved, thanking him and offering to meet up at a later date.

In addition to Osgood's text, he had several angry texts from his father. Smiling at the prospects of the next step in his life and the answers the evening had brought him, Alex looked to the clearing road leading out of the town square. He returned home, a changed man ready to progress to the next step in his life.

S.A. BALLANTYNE

Sea-Side City

Untold Legend

Untold Legend

Cover photo sourced from:
Pixabay

Originally uploaded by:
Pexels

Vector art uploaded by:
OpenClipart-Vectors
&
Clker-Free-Vector-Images

UNTOLD LEGEND

Michael sat in his motorised wheelchair streaming a local wrestling show over the internet. He wished he could be there in person, as the event was only a 15-minute drive away. However, his car battery had died; furthermore, Michael had learned that he couldn't rely on taxis to accommodate his wheelchair during busy periods.

Michael's frustrations increased at the poor quality streaming caused by the torrential rainfall outside.

Even though he was disappointed he couldn't be there in person, there was only one thing Michael wished he could do more. He always wished that he could be a wrestler himself. Sadly, due to his condition, it was impossible.

He had reached a point in his life where he had come to accept it and still appreciated the entertainment it brought him. Michael's frustration was interrupted…

"Love in a mug?"

His annoyances passed after his trusted live-in carer Bernadette brought him some hot chocolate, served at the perfect temperature. Drinking the hot chocolate, Michael felt its warmth spreading to his mind as he started to enjoy the pixelated stream once again.

One of his local favourites, Ian "Pale Horse" Stallion, made his entrance to high volume techno music booming through the community centre speakers.

Ian Stallion's high-risk, entertaining style epitomised Michael's dreams of becoming a wrestler. Bernadette sat back down, pleased with the rejuvenated sense of joy visible in her client's eyes as he continued to watch. She wasn't a big fan of wrestling. This was a product of her predominantly male family being so engrossed with it in her younger years.

However, she had been a carer for several years and had started to appreciate it again, after witnessing the enjoyment it brought Michael.

To Michael's surprise, he could see there was something missing from Stallion's performance. Even through the intermittent connection of his computer screen. Something within Ian's body language suggested he wasn't happy. An average fan probably wouldn't have noticed. But Michael was perceptive when it came to people's emotions and traits, as well as a being a huge wrestling fan.

Michael was irritated to see that Ian's match didn't last long. During the bout, the ring had suddenly become swarmed with other wrestlers and Ian's match had been ruined. This was a planned event to gain popularity for the promoter's favourite wrestler Dave Hex.

Hex would come down and clear the wrestlers out of the ring, allowing him to gain popularity with the audience. Although it was planned, the overly enthusiastic group of young wrestlers had swarmed the ring before they were supposed to. This angered Ian. Michael could tell by Ian's body language, when he saw the wrestlers he was surprised and annoyed by their poorly-timed interruption. However, it was impossible for Michael to know the true depths of Ian's dissatisfaction and the ongoing tension that had being brewing in his life.

Meanwhile, back at the community centre, Ian's boiling point had been reached. After wrestling for Unlimited Pro Wrestling (AKA UP-Wrestling to local fans) for over a year the combination of his injuries and frustrations with politics had consumed him with rage. Distracted by his thoughts for a second, Ian was kicked in the face.

The kick sent him over the ropes and out of the ring, landing awkwardly and hurting his back on the side of the ring. Shaking off the blow and nursing a throbbing eye, he walked off in frustration as planned. However, once he got backstage, Ian decided he would leave.

Quietly making his way through the cramped changing room the wrestlers were using, Ian collected his gym bag. Undetected by his peers, he left the building and set off for home.

He zipped up his hoodie and put his hood up to protect him from the harsh, cold, damp fog the October night provided. There were still a couple of hours before the show finished, so the street was free from loitering fans looking to meet the wrestlers. Wandering down the street, Ian admired the beige glow of the old street lighting, which illuminated his journey home through the chilling mist.

Ian's body was battered and aching from head to toe; he had endured a number of injuries which had accumulated through his years of wrestling. This was further aggravated by the stress Ian was under, constantly feeling he was being held back. Contemplating what he had wanted to achieve in the wrestling business and how it paled in comparison to what he had done so far, he felt a sense of hopelessness. However, what he didn't realise at that time was that his frustrations stemmed from something far deeper.

Finally making it home to his mother's house, Ian felt physically and mentally exhausted. At this point, the swelling around his eye where he'd been kicked was starting to become more visible. Luckily his mother was out for the evening. Ian didn't want to face another one of her lectures about not having a proper job, so he decided to go to bed before she returned.

Michael was still enjoying the rest of the show on his computer. Once it had finished he was inspired to play with his games console; eager to recreate what he had seen on the show on the latest Live Action Wrestling game. LAW (Live Action Wrestling) was the premier brand of professional wrestling, known around the world.

The vast majority of wrestling fans and independent wrestlers across the globe had deep desires to be a part of LAW, from trainees like Ian to seasoned veterans of the craft.

Although Michael accepted that an in-ring career would be impossible, he loved the freedom to be able to get lost in the creativity and fun of the video game. In addition to gaming, he also had plans to design action figures and models of the rings and arenas. Furthermore, Michael had generated an impressive online following eager to buy his merchandise. The idea for his creative business originated through his blog where he shared his opinions on the local and international wrestling scene. A couple of hours passed and Michael felt ready to get some sleep. Bernadette helped him into bed.

Sometime later, Ian was rudely awoken by the screeching sound of a passing train, and an excruciating pain in his injured back. The startling sound of the train caused Ian to further aggravate the injury to his back. Exhaling sharply, Ian sat up clasping his bruised body as the noise of the train died down.

His muscles were sore and tense as the cold air had enveloped the room. Looking at his clock, he saw the time was 6AM. Once his initial grogginess had passed, Ian realised it was pitch black outside.

Furthermore, he realised that the summer had slipped by and it had not been as productive as he had hoped. After a few moments, Ian remembered that he was scheduled to attend an interview at the job centre at 9:00 that morning.

"No point staying in the sack now, I'll only sleep in," he said to himself, as he got out of bed, stretching and yawning.

Snoring could be heard from his mother's room down the corridor. In an effort not to wake the sleeping dragon; Ian took his clothes into the bathroom and quietly got washed and changed. He noticed his face had been heavily bruised from the kick he had received the previous night.

"That's going to look great at the job centre," he sarcastically thought to himself, before getting dressed, picking up the last £5 he had left to his name and leaving the house. Closing and locking the door quietly, Ian stopped to admire his car before he made his way down the bitterly cold street.

He didn't have enough money to maintain it properly and he had no money for petrol. His lack of income and transportation had seriously affected his opportunities in the wrestling business.

Ian's attention was drawn to his reflection in the car window as he wiped off the morning dew with his gloves. His entire image had been changed to fit the gimmick that Den wanted him to wrestle under.

Ian had a pale complexion, steely blue eyes and chiselled features. The promoter for UP-Wrestling had encouraged him to dye his hair a vibrant blonde and be clean shaven when he was booked to wrestle. This gimmick came to pass when Ian had arrived at a training session with the dye in his hair from a party the night before.

Den thought he looked like "Party-Starter Carter" an LAW wrestler from a few years back, so he decided to try and replicate the gimmick with Ian to attract the Party Starter's fan base.

Ian, being awestruck about being in a wrestling ring and training with real professional wrestlers, was very compliant with the promoter Den and the trainer's advice and suggestions. He didn't want to appear disrespectful or ruin his chances of getting put on shows in front of live crowds. Ian had tried to explain his own ideas for a gimmick; however, once he was given the gimmick, Den insisted he keep it. Luckily, he had managed to get his name changed to "Pale Horse" before he started to appear on shows as one of the more established wrestlers endorsed the idea. However, the rest of the gimmick stuck, with the upbeat techno music and constant clapping to get the crowd more involved. As time progressed, he was starting to get more and more beaten up. Between the physical punishment he endured on a nightly basis and the frustration of being unable to be creative with his character, Ian had decided his dream was no longer worth pursuing. His solemn stare into his own reflection was interrupted by the steam emerging from his breath.

Ian left his redundant car and made his way towards town to apply for Jobseeker's Allowance. He had dropped out of his college course and he didn't have a penny to his name anymore. Despite his local popularity, Ian never got paid for his wrestling shows. Furthermore, he knew it was bad form to talk about payment with his fellow wrestlers. It was an unspoken rule of the ages for wrestlers not to discuss their earnings. This was especially the case in the earlier years of their career, as it could be perceived as disrespectful or arrogant amongst their peers. The more he stared at the car the more he started to relate it to his own feeling of redundancy. In theory, both Ian and the car could get anywhere in life. However much like the car, without the appropriate fuel and funding, neither he nor the car could go anywhere.

Ian was slowly brought out of his reflective trance as the cold misty wind reminded him of the harsh realities he still had to plough through. Living in the north end of the town, Ian set off on his lengthy journey to the town centre. The main road was still illuminated with street lighting as the nights were becoming longer. As Ian progressed further towards his destination, through his uncharacteristically empty hometown, the sun began to emerge.

Eventually he reached the town centre at around 7AM, wandering through the eerily quiet town square. The gradual increase in daylight had started to lighten Ian's dusky perspective on life. To his pleasant surprise Ian found that Coastal Collage, the town's primary indoor shopping centre, was open.

None of the shops inside were open. However, the venue provided much needed warmth. Furthermore, the futuristic design and therapeutically coloured lighting of the building's interior presented Ian with a tranquil environment to relax in before his interview at the job centre.

Although he was predominantly a creature of the night, he was starting to see the value of an early start. Walking across the smooth, slick, snow-like flooring; Ian found an empty seat outside one of the main shops. Sitting on the bench and enjoying his surroundings, he started to think about what sort of jobs he wanted to apply for. Whilst he was an athlete, Ian had sacrificed a lot of potential qualifications in pursuit of his dream. Alas, this didn't make him very employable, despite being an intelligent young man.

Moments turned to minutes and minutes turned to an hour. The day gradually started to show signs of life, the number of people circulating the area started to increase. Noisy school children and commuters picking up snacks and drinks before work brought Ian back into the realms of reality. Coming to, he searched the smooth, futuristic retail outlet for a clock. Discovering it was 8:40, it was at that point Ian noticed that the lighting subtly blended into different colours as the hours of the day passed.

Emerging from his seat, Ian was reminded of how injured his body was. None the less, he collected his thoughts and proceeded to the local bakery to get himself breakfast. £5 wouldn't get him far in this day and age in Britain, but it did get him a sausage roll, an orange juice and a doughnut.

Once his breakfast was concluded, he made his way out of Coastal Collage and braved the brisk morning which awaited him. He took the short walk down the precinct to the Job Centre under the bleak, dull overcast grey sky.

Approaching the Job Centre, Ian noticed three elderly

men sat on a bench peering in the triple glazed glass walls. As he drew nearer, it became obvious there was a commotion unfolding.

"You thieving bunch of... I need my money!" A disgruntled thug in a tracksuit yelled as he was being frogmarched by two security guards and an excitable man in a shirt and tie.

The man shrieked:

"Mr Scott! You have failed to provide sufficient evidence that you've been looking for work or are medically incapable of doing so. You've left us no choice but to cut your Jobseeker's Allowance."

The thug strutted angrily; muttering curse words in rage, protesting "I've got a family to feed you mongs!"

The security guards stood between the thug and the member of staff. They pushed him away in self-defence, ordering him to leave the area before they called the police. Ian was standing no more than 15 feet from the centre and was bemused at the disturbance before his eyes.

"What the hell am I walking into" he thought to himself. Nonetheless, he made his way into the building. He passed the two security guards at the door, who were looking on disapprovingly as the thug started arguing with the three old men sitting on the bench.

Ian unzipped his hoodie and pulled down the hood, adjusting his body temperature to the stifling air conditions in the building. He overheard a conversation between the man who hid behind the security guards and one of his colleagues.

"I ought to have wrung his neck. How are we supposed to get people like that into a job? Utter scumbag!"

Ian waited in anticipation, till their conversation had concluded. "Yes?! What can we do for you?"

The man shrugged, avoiding eye contact with Ian in an unprofessional manner. Ian introduced himself and explained he had an appointment with a Mr Robert Richardson.

"Ah yes, that's me. Come through to my office."

Mr Richardson replied, beckoning Ian to follow him.

Ian felt as though he was back at school seeing one of the onsite career advisers. He had never really found the advisers he had encountered very useful. They all seemed to be pleasant people who were happy to discuss various different career paths, they just didn't listen to what he truly wanted. Despite his previous experiences however, he followed Mr Richardson through to his office.

Once they sat down, Mr Richardson noticed Ian's black eye, which had swollen in the cold.

"What on earth has happened to your face?"

As Ian started to explain his unpaid wrestling career, one of the elderly men from outside barged into the office. "That ruffian outside is threatening us!"

Mr Richardson erupted with irritation

"Where's the security guard? Sir, please get out and talk to the security guard!

As for you Mr Stally: being a wrestler obviously isn't working out for you if you have no income and you're looking for work with a battered face from a fake sport."

Following Mr Richardson's rant, the old man at the door left the room chuckling:

"Professional wrestler, ha-ha that boy's a weed, wait till I tell Nigel."

Ian started to feel angry at how he was being treated by both Mr Richardson and the old busybody.

Silently seething, he could feel his head simmering with discontent while Mr Richardson barraged him with his constructive criticism. After being ordered to cut his hair and dress more conservatively, among other things his mother had already told him, Mr Richardson finally agreed to put Ian on unpaid work experience, which entitled him to benefits.

Aware of his financial predicament, Ian had no choice but to smile and be as polite as possible. However, the tension behind his smile almost broke his gritted teeth.

Following one final lecture as a summary of the appointment, Mr Richardson escorted Ian off the premises.

Once Ian got outside, he was welcomed by cheers from the three elderly men on the bench, still highly amused at his claims of being a professional wrestler.

Mr Richardson overheard them and bellowed out of the door at them:

"Haven't you all got something better to do than sit out there all day?!"

Ian put his earphones in as the old men started to answer back. He usually enjoyed a bit of banter; however, he wasn't in the mood due to the morning he was having. Ian plugged his earphones in and drowned out his frustrating surroundings with heavy metal rock music.

Meanwhile, in the hilly outskirts of the town, Michael was in the process of getting up. For a lot of people Michael's age, 9:20 in the morning was no time to be voluntarily conscious, far less getting out of bed. Bernadette was always up and dressed beforehand in anticipation of getting him up. As a seasoned carer, she had grown accustomed to Michaels's routine and knew him very well.

Like most people, Michael went through different phases in life.

At this time, he was highly motivated, enthusiastic and passionate about getting things done to help his business ideas develop.

It took time for Michael to get dressed and into his chair and he didn't want the morning to escape him. He would wake up at 8 AM, allow himself an hour to sit in bed and check through the internet on his phone with a hot chocolate. The internet served as a morning newspaper for Michael, he liked to be up-to-date with what was relevant in the wrestling world, which allowed him to develop his ideas and drum up business from potential customers.

Concluding his morning routine, Michael was wide awake after a couple of hours.

"Has that bloody battery arrived yet?"

Within a few moments of Michael's irritated question, a man came to the door to deliver his car battery.

As Bernadette went out to fit the battery, Michael exclaimed: "Have I won a bloody million pounds yet?"

Checking his bank account through his phone he sighed:

"Well, it was worth a try."

At the other end of town, Ian had just arrived back at the Stally household.

"Oh, for heaven's sake Ian! WHAT HAVE YOU DONE TO YOUR FACE?"

Ian's mother shrieked. She continued in her signature, high pitched, harpy like tone:

"It's no wonder he gave you a hard time, you've dropped out of education, you've got no work experience and you turned up with a face like a butcher's counter! They must have thought you were a common thug."

Ian didn't have the energy to argue with his mother as his day had been a constant barrage of headaches and body aches. Leaving the house, Ian went for another walk in an attempt to escape the negativity, trying desperately to get himself back to the peaceful frame of mind he was in at the Coastal Collage. Suddenly Ian's evasive train of thought was interrupted by his phone vibrating in his pocket.

Answering it, he was informed that he would start work experience in Lou's News. The shop was but a five-minute walk from his house. Drawing the one sided conversation to a close, Mr Richardson ended the phone call by encouraging Ian to sort his hair out.

"Hmm, work experience. At least that's something."

Ian thought to himself, brushing his hair back.

A few days later, Ian started his work experience at Lou's News. He arrived at the store, with his hair still not cut, but he had washed the dye out. Upon his arrival, Ian was greeted by a short plump lady named Lou, the store manager and tenant of the property above. She was pleasant, but loved a good gossip; her beady little eyes would light up with excitement every time she got a whiff of something to talk about. Unsurprisingly, once she found out Ian was a wrestler; she couldn't wait to tell him her views on wrestling when it was on the television back in her day...

"And you had Big Ben; he was a huge big thing. He used to have them right up on his shoulders and slam them backwards. Of course those were the days before all those Americans started making it ridiculous."

Ian was tuning in and out of the conversation as he had heard it all before. He kept his opinions to himself, though it did amuse him that a number of adults he'd met believed that the old British wrestling was real, simply because of its lack of story orientated content.

Eventually he was left to his tasks of restocking the shelves. Although the shop was primarily a newsagent, Lou stocked a number of different products including arts and crafts equipment. Ian started to stock up the shelves. As the day progressed he started to find solace in his work.

It was quite a quiet day for business; when Lou had gone on her lunch break, Ian was trusted to man the tills and look after the shop. He felt reassured by this because it showed that he had earned Lou's trust in the short time they had worked together. Shortly after Ian had been left in charge, Michael and Bernadette entered the shop.

Michael had come to pick up equipment to make a model wrestling ring in an effort to make local online sales to younger fans.

To Michael's delight, he recognised Ian at the till; he sped over to him in excitement:

"IAN STALLION!?"

He exclaimed in surprised delight, by this point Ian had

started to glow with embarrassment and surprise.

"I'm trying not to be at the moment. How can I help sir?"

Ian replied, trying to conceal his bitterness towards his ring name. Unfazed by Ian's attempt to calm him down, Michael continued to bombard Ian with unwanted attention regarding his former identity.

With each excitable sentence, Ian could feel his breathing start to increase as he tapped the counter while his frustration built. Bernadette could see the blushing negativity circulating Ian's pale complexion. She quickly interjected and told Ian what her client wanted from the shop and redirected the conversation to what they were going to do with them:

"I know it sounds like a weird combination, but we're going to try and build a wrestling ring."

Ian's mood was lightened by Bernadette's conversational diversion; he jokingly replied:

"You'll need a lot more than we've got in stock to make one of them,"

Michael went on to explain to Ian how he was going to make cheap and endurable wrestling toys and play sets to sell within their local community.

His business plan and positive attitude inspired Ian and made him realise how his negative mind-set may have been keeping him from achieving what he wanted in life. The irritation and bitterness had slowly drifted from his mind; Ian took the opportunity to properly introduce himself to Michael and Bernadette. After a brief conversation they left the shop and Ian carried on with his days' work.

When Ian arrived home that night he checked through his various forms of social media on his ancient home computer with the comfort of a freshly brewed hot chocolate. He'd lost touch with most of the friends he'd made at college as a result of the anti-social habits he'd developed through his training routine. To his surprise, he had received a friend request from Michael on Open-

Options.

Instantly confirming Michael's identity through the LAW logo he used as a profile picture, he accepted the request. Ian looked through Michael's information and photos. He started to appreciate how much the young man had accomplished.

The front door quietly opened as Ian's father made a rare appearance at the house. Undetected by Ian, who was deep in thought at his computer, his father poked his head around the door frame.

"Hello son, how are you doing?"

He stage-whispered. Ian turned round and welcomed his father. He hadn't seen him in a while owing to the breakdown of his parents' marriage. After a brief catch-up, Ian's father's attention was drawn to the computer screen.

"Who's that?"

He asked referring to Michael's profile.

"Ah a wrestling fan I met earlier today,"

Ian replied.

William Stally scoffed, "You're still into the play fighting then?"

Their conversation was interrupted by Ian's mother:

"William? What are you doing here?"

Before their next fight broke out, Ian quickly returned to his computer and plugged his earphones in. Blocking out the ruckus with his classic '80s metal playlist, he went back onto Open-Options to find he'd received a message from Michael asking if he'd be wrestling on the next local show.

Ian welcomed the distraction from his parents' arguing in the next room. He explained to Michael his predicament; Ian, like so many other wrestlers, tried to keep fans away from his personal life. However, with the way his life was going at that point, Ian appreciated that he needed friends and was humbled enough at that point to confide in Michael.

He explained how he had to stop wrestling to make his way in life, and aired his grievances about how things were going. As the conversation progressed, Michael invited him to watch the next UP-Wrestling show with him. Ian agreed as his Jobseekers Allowance would be in by the end of the month.

Within a few weeks, after several days of work, several online conversations with Michael and one drastic haircut, Ian had come to terms with the changes in his life and started to be in a more positive mind set as the night of the show arrived.

Bernadette picked Ian up in Michael's car and the three of them set off to the local community centre where UP-Wrestling hosted their shows. Ian helped Bernadette get Michael out of the car, which impressed her because most people had stood around awkwardly waiting in the past.

Once they were all ready and out of the car, Ian noticed the promotional posters outside the arena which simply read Live Wrestling. This started to remind Ian of his grievances with the way things were run at UP-Wrestling. One aspect which had attracted both Ian and Michael to the world of wrestling was the creativity and panache with which it was presented.

Both Ian and Michael agreed as fans that wrestling shows should be advertised with a creative title to attract an audience. This was especially the case for an event on bonfire night, and they discussed potential titles for the event on their way to the seating area. However, Ian knew that the promoter Den was a stubborn man and he didn't take kindly to ideas from fans or trainee wrestlers.

Once they arrived at the seating area, Ian saw a familiar face. His old friend and seasoned wrestler Pete came over to greet Ian.

"How are you doing stranger? Where's the barnet gone?"

he asked Ian, shaking his hand.

Michael glowed with excitement. Pete quickly noticed

and put his finger to his lips; preventing his star-struck fan from blurting out his ring name and drawing attention to him.

After a brief catch-up with Ian, Pete drew his attention to Michael and asked him his thoughts on his character. Michael started giving him ideas for different move sequences in his matches. Pete quickly retrieved a small note pad and pen from his combat trouser pockets and jotted down Michael's ideas, saying:

"Thank you for the ideas my friend. People like you keep me alive in there.

If the ideas are good, then give the people what they want.

I'll hopefully see you guys later if not somewhere down the road. Don't forget to cheer for X-Tension out there; I heard he's wrestling an evil pirate."

Bernadette chuckled at Pete/X-Tension's maverick personality "He's a smooth one," as he jogged backstage, putting away his note pad.

A few moments later the show started. Den made his way down to the ring as the master of ceremonies for the event. Seeing him strut down to the ring in a pinstripe suit, with slicked back greasy black hair resembling an aspiring 1920s mobster made Ian remember how arrogant the man was.

Trying to conceal his disdain, Ian cheered as the show started. The opening contest was a women's match featuring local favourite Boudica, who was a member of the Sea-Side Saxons of Penelope Park.

Standing at 6 feet tall, she was dressed in a brown leather corset, wool tights and boots and sporting war paint, a sheepskin coat and a re-enactment spear. She was an impressive sight to behold. The roar of excitement she invoked from the crowd helped Ian remember what attracted him to wrestling, allowing him to forget his troubles and enjoy the show. The match was over in record time as Boudica finished her puny opponent with her signature swinging butchers grip reverse bear-hug.

His enjoyment would come to an end during the interval when he was beckoned over to the merchandise table by Den. Ian went over to him, shuffling around the huddle of people haggling around the table. Looking perturbed, Den ushered Ian away, out of earshot from the crowd.

Seething, Den questioned:

"Where have you been? And what the hell did you do to your hair? We've been working together for a year and you just disappeared for a month and ruined your whole gimmick. No one is going to know or care who you are now!"

Ian started to feel bad. Although he didn't like Den much, he started to realise that he hadn't contacted him to tell him his situation yet. He apologised and tried to explain his financial dire straits, but Den interrupted:

"I don't care, we've all got problems pal.

I gave you a shot in this business and you disrespected us. When you do come back, you're going to have to work very hard to get back in my good books."

With his closing words, Den slicked back his greased hair and slipped behind the curtain.

Stricken with anger, regret and confusion Ian tried to come to terms with his volatile emotions once more, while returning to his seat. Michael and Bernadette could tell something was bothering Ian on his return, but they weren't quite sure what it was. He was as polite as he could be to them, but he was quiet and an atmosphere had formed.

Shortly after, the show resumed. The next match of the evening was a tag team match, featuring Sid "The Wild Kid" Cassidy; the head trainer at Den's wrestling school. Ian was happy to see his former teacher in action; however, his stomach started to churn as he heard Dave Hex's entrance music hit.

Den was promoting Hex as a hero to the fans. However, his arrogant attitude partnered with his foul temper aimed at trainee wrestlers and aspiring fans was far from the heroic image he and Den were trying to portray in the shows.

In amongst the cheers of the fans, Dave Hex revealed his true personality sneering at the sight of Ian at the ringside. The glance was subtle enough to remain undetected by anyone else in attendance, but it was enough to make Ian's blood boil. For the sake of his new found friend however, Ian decided to grin and bear it.

Towards the conclusion of the match, Hex hit his signature submission manoeuvre: "The Hexagram".

Ian could tell by the angle that his opponent's body was being contorted, that Hex was intentionally hurting the young rookie he was working with. As the rage filled Stallion's eyes, Sid Cassidy turned and pointed to Ian, smugly drawing the crowd's attention to him shouting "This should have been you!"

The crowd, which included a large number of excited young children, started to laugh and make fun of Ian and Michael.

Speechless with rage, Ian saw the sheer embarrassment on Michael's face due to the unwanted attention. Despite knowing it was Sid's way of trying to encourage him to come back to wrestling and potentially set up a storyline, Ian was ready to explode with rage.

The adrenaline pumping through his veins causing his limbs to shake, he finally rose from his seat shouting back at Sid "You think this is fair on him?!".

Being used to dealing with unpredictable situations in her line of work, Bernadette intervened, pulling the fired up Stallion away from the ring.

"I think it's time we all left now." Bernadette advised Ian, while signalling for Michael to follow them to the car.

With that, the testy trio took their leave, Hex encouraging the audience to sing an insulting song about

Ian's new haircut.

Reaching the front car park, fireworks were lighting up the sky. Still enraged and oblivious to their beauty Ian kicked the community centre wall. Michael felt traumatised by the rush of unwanted attention, exclaiming:

"I'm starting to see why you don't want to go back there!"

Ian growled:

"UP-Wrestling? They should be called UP-Den's…"

Bernadette once again made a timely interjection, undoing her ponytail and releasing her long brunette hair:

"Okay boys, I think we need a change of scene to lighten our mood. How about we all go to your favourite pub Michael? Come on Ian I'll buy you a drink, it's not far from here."

Michael started to smile again; he had a feeling he knew what Bernadette had planned.

A short walk later, they reached a pub named the "Port in a Storm". The three friends entered the bar, Ian still irate following the events from the show. He approached the bar at speed passing an elderly man with long scraggy hair and a dark green jacket. Ian ordered a lager to pacify his rage.

Michael, on the other hand, was in much better spirits and eager to discuss the evening's events. Bernadette followed behind the two lively lads, greeting the man sat at the bar as she passed. The man behind the bar nodded to Bernadette as he poured Michael his drink. Although Ian hadn't been to the pub before, the man behind the bar seemed strangely familiar.

There was another middle-aged gentleman sitting on a stool at the other end of the bar, his solemn face staring into oblivion as he poured alcohol down his throat. It was evident the man was a heavy smoker due to the pleasant blend of booze, smoke and aftershave that emanated from his aura.

However, at that moment, Ian was only interested in his pint. Michael asked Ian if he was going to wrestle again. Stopping mid-swig, Ian slammed his pint to the bar replying:

"After what they just did to us?! They can go to hell!

I spent my whole life watching arseholes like Dave Hex, thinking they were amazing,

when in reality they're just a face for a conman like Den to bleed the fans dry!"

After Ian's outburst, a husky old voice from across the bar interjected:

"Good lord kid! Get a grip. It's not easy for a promoter to sell tickets to watch a couple of men in tights prance about the ring! You've been doing it what, a year? You're probably just upset because you're sore and they're not paying you yet. Bloody typical!"

Just as Ian was about to respond to this unknown patron's onslaught of judgement, an incredibly large figure darkened the doorway behind the bar.

"Ay up, what's going on here?"

the giant man bellowed.

"Big Ben! This is Ian, the wrestler I was telling you about," Michael announced.

Ian's jaw dropped in shock as he adjusted his eyes to the ginormous, world-renowned wrestling legend and former national treasure that stood before him. Lost for words and trying to take in the vast and varying changes, Ian contemplated the emotional rollercoaster of a night, as the free-for-all conversation at the bar continued.

Big Ben joked:

"Maybe Jasper over here could be your new manager Ian."

The agitated man snarled:

"Bugger off Ben! This weed doesn't even know he's been born!

The business used to keep little twerps like him out, now there's an infestation of the flying vermin!"

Laughing at his long-time in-ring comrade Jasper and his predictable short temper, Ben explained the fallen star's back story.

"Old Jasper over here is the epitome of how bitter professional wrestling can make someone. It's not without valid reason though. He was the finest wrestler in the country back in the '70s. Then, about a decade later when I broke in, Jasper got pitched a deal to come and wrestle in America.

So naturally he hopped on a plane to Dixie. A couple of months later the regional televised promotion he was working for was bought out and he was left high and dry somewhere in the Nevada desert. A couple of years later when I was making it big, I found him out there and paid for him to come home."

Jasper growled:

"You still can't work as well as I could in the ring. You're just big!" He belched as his head slumped into his arms.

Looking on, with a hint of sorrow in his face, Big Ben instructed the barman:

"Ok, he's had enough for tonight, let's set him up on the sofa out the back."

Ben turned to Ian as he helped the barman carry the passed out Jasper Flint.

"The sad thing is he's right, but he didn't need to let himself go the way he did. When I get back, you and I are going to have a proper conversation, if you're still here."

As the two men carried Jasper out into the back of the pub, Ian turned to Bernadette and Michael asking:

"Ok, what's going on here?"

The two friends started to giggle as their social experiment was becoming more obvious.

Shortly after, Ben returned and bestowed his seasoned and insightful knowledge upon Ian:

"Now, I understand you've had your grievances with

the business and some of the less than admirable people in it. I'm not going to lie to you kid, it's not meant to attract people.

For a great many years the wrestling circle would actively deter people for a number of reasons. I guess what I'm trying to say is, however bad you've had it, and whatever kind of a raw deal you think you've got, there's always someone who's paid far more of a price to keep the business alive. People no one has heard of have been crippled, had their personal lives destroyed and even died, pursuing their arguably insane wrestling dreams.

Unless someone sees wrestlers in the ring giving it 110%, then there won't be a tradition to carry on anymore.

Michael's shown me your matches Ian, and you have potential. Millions across the world who fall in love with our business would kill for it. There's going to be a lot of bully boys, ego maniacs and conmen that you'll meet along the way. But if you turn on your heels and give up now, you'll only appreciate what you've got when it's too late. You don't want to be like the shell of a man who's passed out drunk on my living room sofa do you?"

Ian felt humbled at the inspiring wisdom he had received from the soulful giant of a man. As Ian reflected on his epiphany, taking in the vast emotional changes of the night, Big Ben drew his attention to Michael:

"Anyway, how's your business coming along Mr Stanley? Have you made an action figure of me yet? I'd better look handsome."

Michael laughed and started to explain his masterplan:

"When I do make action figures you'll be the first one I make. But it's quite an expensive process at first with all the materials and equipment I need. I'm starting off by creating a cheap but endurable ring playset, it's universally appealing to young wrestling fans worldwide and it'll be easy to make a profit and compete with the ridiculously overpriced LAW playsets."

Ben's face lit up as he excitedly grabbed the portly

barman by his shoulders, almost causing his glasses to fall from his face:

"Are you hearing this Jimmy?! That's brilliant mate. If you need anything to help you with that let us know.

I'm so proud of you kid, I always knew you were a bright one as a young'un but you've got all the makings of an entrepreneur! Keep on keeping him safe Bernie; you're doing a great job."

Ian started to realise that he was in the presence of greatness from both the past and the future.

An established legend in Ben and quite possibly one of the most inspirational and brightest young people of the future in Michael. In amongst the positive atmosphere, he started to feel ashamed at what little he had done to improve his future up until this point.

Jimmy the barman, approached Ian quietly while Michael, Bernadette and Ben toasted the future.

He slipped his business card across the bar; the card simply read 'Jimmy Bennett − booking agent' with a contact number and email address.

Having overheard Ian and Ben's conversation, Jimmy reassured Ian:

"I can appreciate you may have heard some tall tales before on the wrestling circuit, but I can assure you, my old man's words hold as much weight as his stomach does. Give me a call if you want back in. I'm sure we can work something out for the future. Get yourself sorted first and we'll see what's what."

Ian nodded in appreciation of the opportunity and took the card. The night drew to a close soon after. Expressing how much he had enjoyed meeting Ben and Jimmy, Ian took the inspiration and motivation he had gained through their company back into his reality.

Early the next morning Ian woke up revitalised and ready to make a difference to his life. His body felt better than it had for quite some time owing to the period of rest he had undertaken. Vaulting out of bed, he felt a rush of energy push through his chest.

He looked to the floor of his room and noticed his weight set stacked on his beige carpet.

Although it was still bitterly cold outside, Ian decided the best way to use this newly-found positive energy was to start exercising again. Stretching out, Ian started to warm up before picking up his dumbbells. He worked his way through the set. After a while he started to exhale heavily, which attracted negative attention from down the corridor.

"What the hell's going on in there? It's not even 7 o'clock!"

His mother had been rudely awoken by his exercise routine and was on the warpath. Reaching the doorway in her dressing gown, her sleep deprived eyes peered through her scowls and scarecrow hair as she waited for an answer.

Ian got his breath back and happily stated:

"I'm going to have another crack at the wrestling business."

His mother shrieked:

"WHAT?! Oh for... the only thing you're going to crack is your back."

She stomped back up the corridor slamming her bedroom door in disgust.

Ian chuckled to himself at his mother's irritation:

"Today's a good day already."

As the morning progressed, Ian did some soul searching and started to develop ideas to help move his life away from the negative cycle he had trapped himself in. He started to jot down ideas. It didn't take him long to realise his finances and list of contacts were limited, to say the least. He didn't want to involve the Bennetts or Michael at this point, mainly because of his pride and the fact that he wanted to rebuild his confidence independently before starting afresh.

Finally, he started to form a plan. Ian had toyed with the idea of going back to college, as he had only dropped out earlier that year and his grades were good. However, being a 20-year old, he may not qualify for Educational Maintenance Allowance.

To compensate for this financial shortcoming, Ian decided to go on a field trip down to Lou's News. Once he had arrived, he managed to negotiate an agreement of part-time employment for weekend work.

Content with his hours of employment, Ian set off to go back home and re-apply for his college course. Suddenly he felt his phone vibrate; Michael was calling:

"Hey Ian, I don't suppose you're free to help my friends move in to their new place today?"

Intrigued by the invitation Ian agreed, making his way to Michael's place, which was conveniently close to Lou's News. Arriving at Michael's bungalow, Ian was greeted by Bernadette who offered him one of her signature hot chocolates while they waited for Michael's friends to arrive. Sitting in the living room, Ian enquired as to how long Michael had been planning his model designing and online business plan.

Michael explained:

"Well, I've loved wrestling for a long time. Obviously I can't get in there and wrestle but that doesn't mean I don't want to be involved in it.

One night I ended up getting into a debate on Open-Options with someone on the other side of the globe about who the LAW champion should be. I'd never met this person, but we had a difference of opinion and he started insulting me personally and making fun of my pictures. I was so angry and frustrated, I had to remove him and go incognito for several months to stop the repercussions.

After a while though, I got over it and then I realised that the internet has a lot of great aspects to it; the only problem is people get brought down, enraged or side-tracked by distractions and 'noise'. There are a lot of opportunities out there if people remain focused on their goals. So I started a web page reviewing different shows and chatting to fans. After a few months of talking to more positive people, I saw gaps in the market. It wasn't long before I developed ideas for a new project to create something positive and constructive."

Ian felt quite moved by Michael's story and had the utmost respect for what he was trying to achieve. He had also noticed how much more confident Michael had become in talking to him once they had got to know each other and Michael's star-struck attitude towards Ian had worn off. Michael further explained:

"The toy-selling business isn't the only thing I've got going either. I've got a plan to launch a website where local fans can interact with each other. Last year I started writing reports on each show I attended so I could archive it and give people visiting the site a backlog to keep them entertained and form discussions of memories at events.

I tried messaging Den about it but he just kept ignoring my messages and being evasive at shows."

Suddenly the doorbell sounded and when Bernadette opened it, in walked Big Ben with his wife, Jimmy and an athletic looking young man in his late 20's. The young man introduced himself as Axle. Big Ben interrupted:

"His real name's Joe by the way but his ring name's Axle Airborne."

Ian enquired why he would forego his family name, to which he replied:

"I love and respect my dad, but he understands that I want to break out on my own and make my own name for myself. Promoters would jump at the chance of booking me under the family name because it would sell tickets. But I wanted to build myself up off my own merit first, so I moved out on my own for a couple of years and got myself booked under Axle Airborne to create my own style."

Ian started to realise that in the midst of what had

happened during his time wrestling, his views had drastically changed and everything that he thought about it had been altered over the course of his training. Although he still felt positive about the future, he started to question what he could truly offer the wrestling business.

Every idea he'd ever had about his character or what he wanted to do had been either shot down and made to benefit someone else at a later date; or ridiculed by Den and his favourites.

Observant as ever, Michael sensed the wheels turning in Ian's mind and encouraged everyone to get the vans set up. Bernadette, Ian and Michael started the car, while the Bennetts loaded themselves into the two vans. Michael soon got to the bottom of what was on Ian's mind, but Ian was more interested in finding out where the Bennetts were moving to.

After a short while, the convoy arrived at a large building, not far from the "Port in the Storm", Big Ben's pub. The building had been an abandoned clubhouse before the Bennett's bought and renovated it. It had taken a lot of work; however, they pulled through as a family, and after months of planning and redecorating it was finally ready.

Entering the clubhouse, Ian noticed an oak staircase at the side of the room which lead to what looked like a large office with windows overlooking the spacious ground floor. His attention was then drawn to the ground floor, where a 16x16ft square area in the centre of the room was marked with tape. Ian started to realise that this clubhouse was being tailored to become a wrestling complex.

As Ian stood in awe of the architectural greatness before him, he felt Big Ben's large hand gently grasp his shoulder:

"This is what it feels like to be in the right place, at the right time in this business. Much like life, there are no guarantees, but just the incentive to make it from one defining moment to the next.

I trust you have experience setting up a ring?"

Ian smiled as they started to set things up:

"I should have known that's what would be in the second van."

Joe exclaimed:

"What are you on about mate? It's in the first van! Priorities!"

Once they got to the ring van, Joe noticed Jimmy sitting in Michael's car eating a bacon sandwich, cosied up in his warm winter coat, his glasses started to steam up with the hot air emitting from the car heating. Visibly frustrated at the display of laziness, Joe marched up to the car and irritably knocked on the window shouting:

"Oi, what are you doing in there! Get your big fat arse out the car and help us set up the ring!"

Startled at his younger brother's outburst, Jimmy rolled down the window and simply said: "Undercard!"

Joe's face dropped at the possibility of being demoted to a less than favourable position on shows by his older brother.

"Our Jimmy's a real grafter. He does have the right idea this time though, you kids go and pay your dues and put the ring up, Bernie will help out too. Feel free to run the ropes or something when it's up. You better have brought some more of those butties boyo." Big Ben laughed as he got in the van with Jimmy, winking at his wife and Michael, who were highly amused at the situation.

As they started to unload the van, Joe grunted:

"It's going to take ages with only three of us."

To Ian's surprise, Bernadette replied:

"Well, we've been doing it long enough, haven't we Joseph! As long as this one can pull his weight it'll be fine."

Astounded at the revelation, Ian asked Bernadette how and why she had been doing it.

She chuckled:

"Damn, I was going to wait till we got the ring set up and give you a surprise cross-body off the top rope. I'm the middle sister; our family doesn't reveal our family connection to avoid unwanted attention.

It's not so bad now but a couple of decades back "Big Ben" was Britain's favourite wrestler. Then he moved to America making big money training some of the LAW wrestlers. I got a bit sick of wrestling over the years. Mainly because of these two fan-boys prattling on about it all the time; I was never a girly girl, but I'd had enough of wrestling being everywhere I looked."

Their conversation continued as they put the ring up. Once the ring had been set up, Ian and "Axle" started to train in it to test it out.

Bernadette started off watching Ian and Joe practicing moves and planning matches. Their creativity and passion not only held Bernadette's attention but reignited the love she once felt for the sport. Before she knew it, she was back in the ring with them getting involved.

Almost an hour passed and the Bennetts and Michael came back into the building to find Ian slamming Joe and Bernadette performing a top rope elbow drop on her brother. Michael's face lit up with amazement, Ben's face was struck with pride and joy.

However, Ben's wife Janet gasped in panic:

"Bernadette Bennett! Come out of there at once, it's bad enough all the men in the family are at it, not you too!"

Jimmy stood brushing the bread crumbs off his green jumper, thinking to himself: "That was alright, yeah, I'd book her."

Bernadette started to glow with embarrassment as Big Ben wiped away a proud tear from his eye while maintaining his British stiff upper lip and casually offering to give Michael and Ian a tour of the building with Jimmy. Bernadette and Joe left the ring to reassure their mother.

The tour of the ground floor led them to discovering a

merchandise area so Michael could sell his products, a bar, and a gym at the back of the building for wrestlers to train. There was also a lift so Michael could have access to the upstairs area.

The upstairs featured an office with a large window for Ben and Jimmy to work in and observe shows from above. Next door to the upstairs office was a large living area where the Bennetts would reside.

Big Ben was visibly excited about what the future held. Standing in the overseeing office, Jimmy explained the plan and chatted to Ian about where he would fit in as they looked down at the ring:

"I'd offer you a seat but we haven't moved much furniture in yet. Anyway, as you've probably gathered this is a complex where wrestlers can train and where we can hold shows which hopefully will attract people from across the country, once word gets out."

Ben interrupted with an enthusiastic outburst:

"And after each show we can all go back to the Port in a Storm for a good old fashioned lock in."

Jimmy continued to explain that if Ian helped them to expand their business and attract trainees and wrestlers on the circuit to work with, he could train with them at a discounted price in return. Ian gladly accepted the offer. He confessed that his views on wrestling had been altered and he no longer knew what persona he wanted to use in the ring.

Jimmy reassured Ian:

"Don't worry about all that, just keep perfecting your craft in the ring and the rest will come with time. All the greats started off doing substandard gimmicks at some point in their career. We can have you wrestle in a mask until you figure out what sort of character you want to portray, that way you can put people over and give you time to grow your hair back too. We'll call you 'Ash' for the time being; once we figure out your gimmick you can lose the mask and rise like a phoenix from the proverbial ashes."

The two agreed to the terms and shook hands before Big Ben invited everyone back to the pub for a celebratory drink.

Once the festivities came to a close, Ian returned home and reapplied for his college course which, in time was successful. Luckily his teachers had gone above and beyond the call of duty to ensure his return, e-mailing him the units he had missed for him to complete before the Christmas break. After tireless hours of work and dedication from both parties, it was arranged for Ian to return to college in January.

Gradually, Ian was building up to his goals through studying, doing part-time work with Lou, and training in the ring at the Bennett's newly-named clubhouse, the Bennett's Wrestling Empire. The Bennett's family goals were coming to fruition as well. After much deliberation, Ben and Jimmy had decided to name their wrestling promotion Bennett's Wrestling Revival. They fashioned a company slogan of "Be Wrestling" under their logo. As the shows started to gain popularity, fans would often chant B... E... Wrestling *clap *clap *clap, in appreciation of the company.

As the months went by, the Bennett's Wrestling Revival gained popularity and quickly became Rockshore's favourite wrestling company. However, Ian was still unsure of what sort of persona he wanted to adapt in the ring. He didn't have a problem performing in the mask and helping other wrestlers gain popularity.

Ian had performed on several shows; he thoroughly enjoyed working with the Bennetts and the wrestlers he was booked to wrestle against, though the generic black mask he was wrestling in and the style he had adapted didn't let him have the same connection with the crowd he had established before (despite Den's best efforts to derail it).

Jimmy and Michael just kept referring Ian to whom his

favourite wrestlers were and encouraging him to watch their matches and to utilize the aspects of their characters which had inspired him when he was young. Ian had always idolised LAW wrestler "London's Finest" Harry Homes; however, he wanted to be entirely original and unique. Unfortunately, it was hard at times to recapture his creativity, due to his previous negative experiences.

Michael had been working tirelessly on a number of different projects; however, Ian was at the top of his list of priorities. Unbeknownst to Ian, Michael had been keeping a journal of Ian's training progress and launched it on his website alongside the Bennett's Wrestling Revival shows. He had done this to generate interest in Ian and create mystery behind the man in the mask. Once Ian's schedule allowed it, they had agreed to meet so Michael could show him his work.

By the time Ian was available to meet up, it was the dawning of spring; the glistening icy roads had cleared and the lingering cold and dark had passed. The skies were clear as warm sunny days re-emerged, mirroring Ian's journey.

Once Ian made it to Michael's house, Michael wasted no time in showing him his journal entries, creatively named "The Stallion's Strides".

Ian was genuinely touched by his friend's efforts and humbled by the resurgent support it had prompted amongst Bennett's Wrestling Revival fans. Then Michael showed him his logo designs, which he'd been creating for Ian's ring costume.

The one that stood out to Ian the most was a horse skull with fire coming out of its mane.

Ian instantly felt connected with the logo design and thanked Michael for his efforts.

Michael played a vignette he had designed, with recorded highlights of Ian's matches with special effects and black and white letters flashing across the screen reading:

"The Dark Horse rides again!"

Noticing how enthralled his friend was at all the work he had put in, Michael picked up his mobile and called Jimmy simply stating: "He's up for it."

Jimmy could be heard at the other end of the phone delighted in his reply: "That's fantastic news! Get him to come down to the Empire and we'll let him know what's what."

Following his creatively productive meeting with Michael, Ian made his way down to the clubhouse. Entering, he found Ben and Jimmy standing in the ring with a third man. Ian's heart started racing as he recognised the man's silhouette. Frizzy brown hair and signature Beige trench coat, the third man was none other than his childhood idol "London's finest" Harry Holmes. As he turned around, revealing his signature goatee and mischievous half smile, Harry noticed Ian's speechless expression of joy

"I trust I don't have to introduce myself, you must be Ian." He said as he hopped out of the ring, shaking Ian's hand. Big Ben chuckled:

"There's a man who still loves wrestling, I haven't seen a face like that since Christmas morning. Wait till you hear the plan son."

Jimmy interjected his usual straight-laced manner:

"The plan is that you will be working as a tag team partner with Harry here to build you up to take the mask off and reveal your new gimmick. It'll be at our show in London around autumn time."

With the help of the Bennett's, his childhood idol and, arguably most importantly, his best friend Michael, Ian had managed to work past all the negativity that had once surrounded him in life, allowing him to achieve his dreams and beyond, to reclaim his childhood passion.

Working among great people to inspire audiences old and new, living in his home country, and revolutionising an untelevised, home-grown wrestling entertainment empire, this story was not an individual achievement, rather a collaboration of great minds and passionate people each drawn together by time and circumstance to achieve something greater than they ever could have done individually.

S.A. BALLANTYNE

SEA-SIDE CITY

Circle of Life

Circle of Life

Cover photo sourced from:
Pixabay

Originally uploaded by:
Hans

THE CIRCLE OF LIFE

Shocked, Cliff gripped his local newspaper tightly as he discovered the obituary of one of his oldest friends. He felt an overwhelming feeling of heart-wrenching sorrow. Being of an older generation and a likely lad of the '60s, he struggled to stop the tears of pain from rolling down his cheeks.

He very rarely saw his friend Fred Smith anymore; however, he had known him for almost 35 years. Sat in his armchair he gazed out of the window at his garden, which had become his personal project in recent years. The sun beamed down on the beautiful green grass and illuminated the old brickwork of the neighbouring house over the garden wall. Cliff was oblivious to the tranquil scenery the sunny Sunday afternoon provided; years of repressed emotion and unfelt sadness had finally caught up with him in one fell-swoop. Cliff was a handyman by trade, and he'd done a lot of work for Fred at mate's rates over the years. Likewise, Fred had done favours for him; they hadn't once fallen out or harboured any ill-feelings toward one another.

He started to recollect other people from that period and how time had passed by and taken or changed them. Although he was saddened by various events that had occurred, he had maintained the proverbial "stiff upper lip" through almost all of it. It was slowly starting to become clear to him, as the minutes turned to hours, that he wasn't just mourning a friend, but a hidden corner of his life as he knew it.

He'd lived in the same town all his life like so many others who resided there. His train of thought took his mind back to vivid memories of the town through the '70s. Although he'd spent a lot of his time working, he remembered various different pubs, nightclubs and shops among other buildings which had all come and gone through the past few decades.

As he'd recollected his life he'd left the confines of his arm chair to reach his small kitchen, where he sought out the comforts of an expensive brandy which he'd been saving for a special occasion. He'd hoped that it would have been a happier one than this, but he was in no position to care.

He heard a creaking from upstairs and the familiar sounds of the floorboards moving in his seasoned Victorian house. His son was slowly descending the stairs. Quickly wiping the tears from his eyes, Cliff cleared his throat, adjusting his voice.

"Henry?! Is that you just getting up?" Cliff enquired.

Henry defended himself against the slur in his high voice "No! I've been up for hours!" and then continued to rant about the quality of the internet on his games console. Henry was quite a large young man, and very defensive about it. His father was unhappy with the way his son was wasting his life away in his room. Usually he dealt with this by creating distance between them and trying to ignore it. But not today. Cliff finally erupted:

"For goodness sake man! It's 3 o'clock on a Saturday afternoon, it's a beautiful day out there and you just shut it out and mess around on that thing up there!"

Henry bellowed back: "What else is there to do? This town's a shi…"

Cliff interrupted "This town's got a lot more to it than the electrical boxes in your room. You don't even . ."

Henry interjected "Oh, here we go!"

Mocking his father, Henry continued:

"You don't even know you're born. When I was your

age I was working."

To Henry's surprise, Cliff spoke in a different tone than he was used to.

"It's not about work. If you went out and won the lottery tomorrow and never had to work again, I wouldn't blame you. This town is something special and you're too wet between the ears to see that or anything past your screens. You're wasting opportunities that no one else has both socially and work-related."

Still being defensive, Henry shrugged "Work opportunities? I didn't even turn up for school half the time. When I did, they sent me home, and the stuff they taught was useless anyway. And socially? Well I talk to people online every day, I was just beating some guy called Tim on Revolution War Games 3 before the server started lagging."

Cliff sighed deeply, cradling his head in his hand.

"You're socially gifted, you can make people laugh, you can wind them up, you can argue any point you want and challenge the way people think. You research things that a lot of people wouldn't know where to start with. That's intelligence that can't be taught in school and a talent that some doctors and top end, white collar professionals don't possess."

Henry started to pay attention as Cliff continued:

"One day, you're going to wake up at my age and wonder where it all went. Everyone does at some point. The difference is, most people have memories of things they've done, places they've been, people they've met, slept with or whatever. At this current point in time, at the age of 25, you are arguably in the prime of your life. What have you done?"

Completely deflated Henry asked:
"What's brought all this on?"
Cliff reluctantly explained:
"One of my friends has just passed, you only met him a

few times in passing and our encounters were so few and far between that you may not even count him as a friend by your standards. But over the years, when life threw me off course, he was there to see me through it. When your mother left and all the lads thought I was sleeping around, I was round his place trying to make sense of life. He never told a soul just so I could save face in public. The truth is, in the 30 years I knew him, I never appreciated how easily life could take him or anyone else in it. Now I look around and see my circle of contacts I built up over the years is slowly coming to an end."

In an attempt to raise his father's spirits, Henry tried to name people he knew who were still alive.

"Look son, everyone I knew from the best days of my life is either dead, out of contact or old. Hell, I can't even remember what I looked like back in those days and this town's changed a lot too, for better or for worse. I can almost place a bet that it will have changed even more so when you reach my age."

Henry tried to convince his father he was happy in his room as he'd already seen all there was to see in the town. Unfortunately, Henry's abrasiveness angered Cliff and made him regret opening up to him about his loss:

"RIGHT! My world is falling apart, but you've yet to even build yours. No job, no friends, no appreciation for the opportunities at your disposal. I used to have my own little network down here; now I'm a stranger in my own town. Watching aimless young people stargazing, to me they're empty shells, but you might be able to become friends with those people and make both your lives better, and I'm not talking about your virtual friends you meet in your virtual reality. Which, by the way, I'm financing!"

Henry became defensive again: "I don't have enough to pay for it. I'm already spent up thanks to last week on Revolution War Games 3."

Little did Henry know his last sentence would be the one to push his father too far. Cliff's whole demeanour changed to rage. He rose from his arm chair and put his steel-toe capped work boots on. Pointing at Henry, he shouted:

"I've tried to talk to you like Fred used to talk to me; clearly it's not working. WHY the hell would you go out and make something of your life when you're sitting here like some sort of kept house pet?"

Cliff paced about in pent-up frustration. As Henry scowled, Cliff continued:

"When I started work it was for food and accommodation. The benefits your generation now take for granted are desensitising you, stopping you from realising your own potential." With his closing sentence, Cliff took a kick at the modem against his brick fireplace, cracking its shell and causing internal damage to the wiring, rendering it useless.

Henry roared: "YOU STUPID OLD PRICK!" His confrontational outburst was quickly shut down by a calculatingly sharp look of aggression Cliff had perfected during his years of national service with the army. In a quiet, seething, chilling, voice Cliff ordered: "Get out of my house and prove to me that you deserve to use this tool."

In a more desperate tone of voice a devastated Henry exclaimed "What was the point of that? I was searching for jobs online."

"Don't you dare lie to me boy. All you've done is play games which, quite frankly, makes a mockery of what my grandparents and parents went through to protect this country! Now, if you go to the library, they have free internet for 30 minutes. The time's limited so it will give you an idea of how to prioritize what you want to do and not waste time. Quite frankly, I don't care what you do today. As long as you do something and get out of the house, we're making progress. But eventually, the limited resources you have are going to run out so keep that in mind."

A flabbergasted Henry grunted as he left the house and slammed the door in frustration. Although Cliff felt a sense of relief after his first meaningful conversation with his son in some time, he broke down in tears after realising he couldn't turn to his lost friend for further advice. If he had done this back when Fred was still alive, he would have been able to get his invaluable counsel on the situation.

Meanwhile Henry was on a journey he couldn't have predicted before the sitting room showdown with his father. Feeling confused and alone, he wandered aimlessly towards town. Being a stubborn young man, he didn't want to go to the library just yet, though he knew he would have to do something to gain employment soon. His father wasn't a man to change his mind or back down once he had made a decision, especially one driven by such anger. He had limited money, but still more than he had let his father know about. He looked through his mobile phone to see what he could do. Although he was taken back with the home-truths he had just been awakened to, it was becoming evident that he had lost contact with most of his friends over the years.

He remembered a couple of his friends used to hang around in Penelope Park a few years ago. With this in mind, Henry thought he'd drop by and see if any of them were still around. He approached the war memorial archway and remembered what his father had said about his grandparents regarding the war. He bowed his head for a few moments after realizing just how many names were on the plaque. His senses were also awakened as he smelt urine and started to notice empty crisp packets among other forms of litter just floating around the area. He then noticed a tramp sitting and drinking.

Henry assumed the tramp in question was responsible for the smell.

"You dirty piece of shi..." the tramp quickly interrupted:

"Oi! Watch your language here. These soldiers had a right to use language like that in the face of battle, but you've got no excuse."

Henry continued, enraged by the dirty sight before his eyes "Where do you get off pissing on a war memorial?!" The tramp replied:

"I don't, I'm sat here having a drink with some of the fallen hero's that my superiors looked up to in my time of national service. Only children and animals piss in public, so it was probably someone your age. Now clear off before I rub your nose in it, you disrespectful little git."

Henry was surprised at the tramp's insightful response. Having learned a short sharp lesson, he continued on through into the park.

He walked up the path, a group of youths aging from early to late teens caught his eye through a clearing in the bushes. Henry noticed that they were sat on the grass in a circle listening to an old man in Anglo Saxon clothing.

The Saxon elder had fully captivated the group, educating them about ancient Anglo Saxon culture.

Stunned at the seemingly random change in Penelope Park, Henry turned his attentions to the rest of the park. To his surprise the entire area seemed to be occupied by Saxons engaging with the public. Finally his attentions were drawn to a large wooden gazebo. A green flag with a beige symbol was flying above the gazebo; the flag appeared to represent a bird's eye view of the park.

Above the gazebo entrance a sign read

"Penelope Park's Sea-Side Saxons".

Henry remembered Penelope Park as a place where he and his school friends would often go to play truant. He didn't enjoy school, but Penelope Park didn't offer much for entertainment. Most of the youths who frequented the park would resort to antisocial behaviour, usually resulting in fights and underage sexual acts in the seclusion the bushes provided.

It was poorly maintained, littered with empty cans of

energy drinks, used condoms and various drug paraphernalia. At night street gangs would fight for occupancy.

Witnessing how the park had transformed from the harsh environment it once was, to a wholesome family friendly safe space, felt very surreal to Henry. He started to wonder what else had changed as he turned onto a side path which led to town. He wondered to himself how he could possibly cultivate the sort of life his father was referring to. Despite how much had changed, learning about Anglo Saxons didn't interest Henry. Instead he found himself yearning for the escapism his internet powered bedroom provided.

Meanwhile, back at the house, Cliff's emotional state had taken its toll on his body and energy levels. To compensate his drained state, he decided to take an afternoon nap. It didn't take long for him to doze off, thinking about how negative the changes to the town seemed despite the leaps and bounds technology had taken since his youth. The evidence for this was substantiated by the complete disdain his son had for the advantages he had at his disposal.

Cliff didn't often dream when he was asleep, while his straight-laced, un-imaginative attitude descended deep into the layers of his sub-consciousness. However, he would soon experience a dream which he couldn't possibly forget.

He started to dream that he was strolling through the town. However, like in most dreams, it was a distorted version of the town. The town he was dreaming of had a mixture of buildings from his childhood (which were no longer in existence) new shops and, even more curiously, sights he'd never seen before (which didn't really exist). As his dream continued he eventually found himself in a care home.

One of Cliff's worst fears was ending up in an old people's home as he saw his independence as a primary element of his manhood. It was unclear whether he was working there or was a resident in the dream. He found himself just sitting in a chair, waiting. All of a sudden, he heard a familiar voice.

"Hello Cliff, how are you?"

It was his recently deceased friend, Fred.

It hadn't yet registered that Fred had died because of the vivid surroundings of his dream, so Cliff casually replied:

"I'm alright mate, how are you? What are we doing here?"

Fred sat back in his chair, as he used to when he and Cliff had their discussions in the old days, even though both he and Cliff were aged as if the conversation was happening in real time.

"I'm at peace," Fred answered, poignantly,

"Though, I sense you are not. I never thought I'd see you in one of these."

It was unclear whether Fred was referring to the care home environment, the dream itself, or even both.

Cliff felt his eyes start to water, even in his dream. Battling the frog in his throat, he asked:

"What's happened to everything Fred? The town's changed, my boy's wasting away. I'm too old in the tooth to do anything."

The conversation was briefly interrupted by a maid who brought Fred a hot chocolate and a bottle of whiskey.

Fred thanked the maid for his drink and told her that Cliff had had enough; he turned his attention back to Cliff and responded:

"Life's happening Cliff."

Sipping his hot chocolate, Fred sat forward as he used to when he was about to engage in conversation:.

"As far as the town goes, temples always turn to ruins. But it can also be perceived that it's a derelict temple which is undergoing expansions, renovations and several other advantageous outcomes. Take a look around. We're in a care home of some sort. You see a waiting room for death and a sign that your manhood has been taken from you. Every moment we spend in here, your mind is looking for more evidence to feed your fear and assume the worst. Other people will see it as a place of comfort and contentment while they get ready for the unknown in a more relaxed setting. This is especially the case if compared to those living out in the working world, those who live alone and those who have no support for their problems. How is your garden project coming along by the way?"

At this point Cliff understood, in whatever capacity, he was definitely talking to THE Fred Smith he had known for so long. He started to register that this was a perfect opportunity to discuss the conversation between him and Henry. In an uncharacteristically irrational manner, Cliff rushed through his account with his son.

"I just want him to do something. But there's nothing I can do to make him! If my father…"

Fred gently interjected at just the right moment and stopped Cliff's garbled story.

"You haven't answered my question about your garden. Relax, Cool Hand Cliff. Remember?"

Cool Hand Cliff was a nickname Fred had given Cliff years back, and that one sentence made Cliff remember how he used to keep his emotions together all those years ago.

Clearing his throat, Cliff maintained his composure and explained how he had nurtured his garden. He gave a detailed account, which took his mind off his emotions.

Once Cliff had finished describing his garden, he had calmed himself down to the extent that he was naturally ready to listen. With a warm encouraging smile, Fred replied:

"You've given me all the pieces. Now I'll show you what there is to see."

Adjusting his posture to speaking mode once again he

continued:

"That garden didn't just grow as soon as you put the water on it and the sun clapped its rays on the earth. Everything that turns naturally good takes time, patience, and well-timed encouragement. Those plants need more than just a good kick up the arse to get them out of the ground to see the light. Now you've seen them turn into what they are today. The sun is a timeless resource. But it doesn't care what it burns or what it nourishes.

You can be a far more valuable resource to your son. Today, you laid the foundation and put the seed in the soil. Now you have to monitor his progress and use the instincts you have, as a man, as a father and, perhaps more importantly, as once a confused, frustrated angry kid who had to make his way in a world that he didn't understand."

Cliff felt himself starting to wake up. He tried everything in his power to stop himself, but he could feel he was losing his struggle.

Fred gave him one last smile with the closing line:

"I'd wager that boy of yours has started growing already, finding new ways to adapt to his new circumstance. If my death has helped another person to evolve, then I can truly rest in peace.

Keep the Cliff upper lip; it's healthier than a stiff upper lip."

A loud ringing, which he thought to be a fire alarm in his dream, awoke him. It turned out to be his old 1970s telephone ringing. Re-orientating himself, he wiped the tears from his eyes as he glanced at the clock. It was half past 6.

In the two hours while Cliff had been in bed, Henry had found a far better way to pass his day. Shortly after walking up the side path from the park to town, he noticed an ice cream shop which he hadn't seen before.

The shiny neon sign above the door read: Cone-ee-Island.

It was quite a new building and Henry hadn't been to

town in quite some time, as he'd had no reason to. In a moment of curiosity, he looked in the window of this new establishment. To his pleasant surprise he noticed one of his friends from school. It took him but a second to recognise him because of his unique mannerisms. The two friends had at one time been quite close, much like his father and Fred. But due to time, circumstances and choices, they had drifted apart before either of them could know how long it had been.

"Oscar?" Henry thought. He entered the shop to see it was set out like a restaurant.

He'd heard about ice cream parlours like this in America, but he had no idea that they even existed in Britain.

"Henry? Hey dude, I haven't seen you in ages. How you been man?"

Oscar said as he spotted Henry.

Henry was taken back by the sudden rush of both nostalgia and the new ice cream parlour.

Trying not to show his surprise, Henry casually greeted his old friend, but secretly hoped he'd be free for a proper catch up. He couldn't help but notice how much Oscar had changed in appearance, yet he still had the recognisable traits of movement, speech, and his slightly goofy smile.

"What you up to these days, mate?" Henry enquired.

Oscar replied: "I'm at uni dude. How about you?" while he looked around at who else was in the shop with a mixture of nervousness and curiosity.

Henry smiled as this was a trait Oscar still retained after so many years.

"Uni? What you doing in here then? And when the hell did we get a Yankee ice cream shop?"

Laughing about how little Henry had changed, Oscar explained how it had been there for about six months, and that he had been meeting his university friends there regularly.

"Trust you to make your meet-up spot an ice-cream shop, and one with a cringe worthy name at that!. This used to be a bakery didn't it?" Henry commented, staying true to his sceptical form.

Oscar returned the compliment with one of his signature jokes which most people remembered him for: "Well, you know what they say about bakery's…. here today, scone tomorrow."

Henry rolled his eyes, although they hadn't seen each other in almost two years, it felt like just yesterday.

"Hey there Oz, who's the new kid on the block?"

a thick New York accent asked. Henry's attention was drawn to a well-groomed, middle aged man in a traditional American white ice-cream apron with the store's logo on the front of it. The man approached the two re-united friends, extending his hand to Henry, "I'm Shane Mahoney, proprietor."

"This is my mate from school, Henry Tomlinson." Oscar told Shane as he shook hands with Henry.

Oscar invited Henry to join him if he wasn't too busy. With that, Shane welcomed his new customer

"Pleasure to meet you Henry, since you're friends with this guy, the first one's on me. What's your flavour?"

With that the two friends sat down while Shane brought them over a couple of his finest ice-cream waffles. Usually it would have cost around £5 for the now internationally renowned Cone-ee-Island dessert. Soon after their brief catch up, Oscar and Henry were joined by Oscar's university friends.

There was Jeremy-Joe Mahoney (JJ) who was Shane's son, Terry who was one of Oscar's class mates and Shelly (who JJ and Terry seemed to be in constant competition for). Although this was a relatively small group, there was a lot of talent and potential for prosperity in their futures.

JJ was studying marketing, which he already had an advantage in through his father's thriving ice-cream business. The rest of the Mahoney family was back in the states running the family business there while his father had moved across the pond to grow his business internationally and help his son in any way he could.

Terry was studying Sociology with Oscar. However, he had been raised selling to the public on market stalls in London, so he had insights into different sides of life too. He dressed in shirts and jeans to try and fit in with the university crowd and not draw attention to the fact he felt out of place with some of the more academic students. He had not only managed to maintain steady grades throughout his course, but had made a small fortune out of his fellow students through improvised sales.

Shelly was a psychology student who took great pride in her chosen subject and was eager to learn as much as she could. Her behaviour could often be considered quite random, and in some situations inappropriate. It even seemed there were borderline traits of insanity at times. She often carried out improvised experiments while meeting new people out and about in public and wrote them up when she got home. Though some of her antics were at times questionable, she could be a lot of fun and had lots of interesting stories to tell. She stood out straight away with her fluffy, vibrantly pink hair; she often dyed it different colours but they'd always be bright and loud, much like her personality. Shelly also wore thick framed glasses.

Oscar's situation hadn't changed a great deal since he was at school, but it had become clearer that his journeys through college and university were slowly but surely moulding him into the man he wanted to become, even if he didn't always know it. He still lived at home with his mother and heavily relied on her to cook and clean.

Although Oscar was aware of this and often made light of it, he was somewhat afraid of change and having to rely on his own abilities. Even though his mother maintained his cooking and cleaning, she was quite tolerant of Oscar's social activities.

Henry was pleasantly surprised with how the day had turned out.

Despite being deprived of his internet privileges; he had found a beacon of social hope. Henry and Oscar relived a number of school memories and stories of their weekend gaming antics from the past, much to the amusement of Terry, JJ and Shelly.

Before it registered how long he had been out, Henry saw it was coming up for 8 o'clock at night. The students didn't care how long they were out for, and each of them had their own means of funding a variety of entertaining options to continue their evening. Henry, on the other hand, didn't have any real money to spare thanks to his gaming endeavours and online purchases. He didn't want the night to end but he knew he didn't have the money to stay out any longer.

Understanding his predicament Terry offered:

"Mate if we go down the chalice I'll buy you a drink. They play crappy head-banging music but it's really cheap. You can always pay me back another time."

Though Terry's intentions were good, he couldn't help seizing the opportunity to try and get a free drink at another point. It was in his nature to see a potential business deal where others would not through courtesy or short sightedness (depending which side of his moral compass you were on).

In an effort to save her new acquaintance from a potential debt, Shelly immediately came up with a counter offer:

"How about we go bowling? I could pay for your first game. No need to pay me back, the pleasure of your company would be payment enough."

Shelly knew by saying this it would prompt JJ to offer to pay for as many games as they wanted in an effort to impress her.

As she suspected, JJ began to offer to pay for both

Shelly and Henry. However, his father interrupted:

"Whoa, check out big bucks over here! You gonna pay for our flights home for the holidays too?"

JJ started to blush as Shelly concealed her amusement at the inadvertent social embarrassment she had caused.

Finally, Oscar had started to realise by Henry's expressions he didn't want to accept money off strangers.

"Bowling sounds right up our alley. I'll pay for you dude, old time's sake."

Henry started to laugh at Oscar's joke (which he wouldn't normally have done). Although each of them offered to financially help him in their own way; Henry's pride didn't want to accept it.

"I'm going to head off home to be honest. Thanks though, and if you guys want to meet up again though here's my number."

The group were slightly disappointed, but accepted that they would see him soon. Henry appreciated their understanding. What he didn't know was Shane could see his pride and he could also see that something was bothering him.

As a former barman, Shane was used to sussing out a variety of different characters. Throughout the afternoon, between customers, he had been watching and listening, and Henry had earned his respect.

As Henry left, Shane shouted after him:

"You're welcome back anytime kid. I don't say that to all my customers."

Henry smiled at Shane and left. He didn't know what he'd be walking into back home, but he had started to understand what his father was trying to tell him earlier. He felt a sense of social inadequacy amongst his new-found friends. It was more than just in terms of money.

Henry had cocooned himself in his room with his virtual life for years. Furthermore, he may well have continued to do so for several years to come if life and fate hadn't driven him from his unnatural habitat.

After years of assuming the worst of life and not looking for or finding anything to the contrary, Henry was finally proven wrong. Although he was pleasantly surprised that there was hope for a better life out there, he started to fear it was too late to achieve it, due to the social disadvantages his reclusive lifestyle had bestowed upon him.

At this point, he didn't know what he could do to make it better. Walking back to his house, he observed other students making their way to the clubs and pubs. In reality they were oblivious to his presence. Sadly, Henry felt that they were judging him, adding to his self-loathing.

He found himself in a difficult position because every solution he could think of seemed either impossible or unappealing in some way.

He arrived home around nine to find his father slumped in his arm chair having uncharacteristically drunk himself into another deep mournful slumber. Henry went back upstairs, instinctively turning on his games console. He soon realised that the internet was still unavailable. By a stroke of luck, he remembered that the neighbours had a wireless internet connection. To his pleasant surprise, it wasn't secure either. Not only did he manage to connect to it, but it was faster than his used to be.

Much like he had before, he soon forgot all about his trouble's in the real world. Losing his awareness of time, before he knew it, it was 4 o'clock in the morning. He started to feel tired so he went to bed, leaving his console on to download something online.

An hour later at 5, Cliff awoke from his alcohol-induced semi-coma. He emerged from his arm chair with a sore head. He felt embarrassed he had fallen asleep in his clothes from the day before.

He climbed the stair case to go and check his boy was alright (as he hadn't seen him all night). Gently pushing the door open, he heard he electrical humming of the console. The screen read "Download in progress, please wait."

And it showed the time at which the download had started.

"Download?" Cliff thought to himself "that requires the internet!" Further observation showed that it had been downloading since 3:57.

Inhaling sharply, Cliff turned to see the silhouette of his son's large frame, bellowing snores from the bed in the corner of the room. Looking at his watch, Cliff chuckled to himself quietly:

"You're going to get a rude awakening in a couple of hours my boy."

After cleaning himself up and having breakfast, Cliff started to do the crossword from the previous day's paper. He avoided looking at the obituary section at this point as he didn't want to face it today. Periodically, he checked the time on the wall clock. This was both to see how long it was taking him to complete the crossword and to assess a fair time to haul Henry out of bed.

Eagerly anticipating the hands reaching 7 o'clock, Cliff arose from his chair once more.

He hurried into the kitchen, reaching for his most endurable saucepans. Ascending the stairs as quietly as possible, Cliff crept towards Henry's room. Ushering the door open, suddenly Cliff banged the pans together repeatedly.

"Get up! Get up! Get up! It's 7AM. This used to be a lie in when I was in the services."

Henry awoke cringing and covering his ears with his pillow shouting all sorts of profanities at his unwanted alarm call. Cliff drew back the curtains exposing Henry to the bright sun the morning provided. Once he was satisfied Henry was awake enough that he wouldn't go back to sleep, he left the room laughing.

"If you're not down there in 10 minutes dressed and ready for the day, I'm coming back in here with ice cold water."

Henry lay in his bed with his hands clasped over his

face, surprisingly awake for someone who had had less than four hours sleep. It dawned on him that his days of sleeping in till the afternoon were not an option for the time being. Once he was dressed he joined his father at the breakfast table, where he had made him some low-fat buttered toast and a cup of tea with a sweetener in it. On the table his father had laid out the extensive job section of the paper.

"Right then lad, crack on."

Cliff encouraged Henry as he looked up, staring gormlessly with his bloodshot, sleep-deprived eyes.

Though he was less than enthused by the job advertisements he was reading Henry circled a couple and lethargically ate his toast. Leaving the table, Cliff sat in his armchair with his cup of tea, adding: "Never mind drawing circles. Rip out the page, get out of the house and look for a damn job! And hurry up about it, I want my paper back."

Following his father's advice, Henry left the house with the torn off paper. As he left the house, the piercing bright sun irritated the back of his eyeballs. The first advertisement that sounded potentially prosperous was a sales position at a local hardware store named Cutting Craft. Following a short walk (which would have been pleasant if he wasn't so tired), Henry arrived at a quaint little shopping precinct, where he found Cutting Craft.

Entering the store, he found a cheerful young man on the till. Though he seemed cheerful to the customers he was serving, shortly after the small queue of customers had left, his body language seemed to suggest he resented his surroundings.

"Alex! Don't stand around doing nothing. The customers have gone now. Tidy up around the till area."

A short man in a shirt groaned in frustration as he strutted to the front of the shop. Henry realised this was the manager of the shop. Before Henry could approach the till, a well-endowed, attractive female had entered, walking straight past Henry and beating him to the till.

"Are you the manager?" she asked.

The man took on a more personable tone while introducing himself to the young lady:

"Yes I'm the store manager Bill McCray. What can we do for you?"

As they shook hands, the young lady enquired about a job opening and offered to hand in her C.V.

"We have an interview slot next week, if you're available."

Bill replied, before taking the young lady's C.V.

The lady quickly confirmed a time slot before thanking Bill as she left.

As soon as she was out of earshot, Bill looked to Alex and made some sort of sly comment to his less than impressed colleague. Though he couldn't hear what he had said, Henry gathered from the sleazy expression on Bill's face and the frustrated look on Alex's face that it was something disrespectful.

Henry checked the job advert again, which read that there were multiple positions available. Encouraged by the relative ease in which the other candidate was granted an interview, he approached the till and introduced himself to Bill, enquiring about a job in a similar fashion.

Bill grimaced and sighed:

"I'm not sure, have you brought a C.V.?"

Henry hadn't written a C.V. and had never been taught how to write one in his school.

"No, sorry mate. I just saw this advert in the paper and came in on the off chance."

Bill sneered:

"That's not how it works in here I'm afraid. You'll have to get yourself cleaned up and go and get your C.V."

Henry could tell from Bill's comment that he was judging him. He could feel himself getting angry as he'd just seen how easily the other applicant had gotten an interview while he was being frowned upon for even trying.

"You gave that girl an interview pretty quick."

Once again, sighing in frustration, Bill defensively replied:

"She'd brought her C.V. and presented herself well, so you'll have to come back another time with your C.V. sir."

Never one to mince his words when he felt he'd been wronged, Henry shouted that the manager was a prick, gesturing his finger as he left the shop.

Although he felt justified in his response, Henry felt disheartened by how he was treated when he had made the effort to apply for a job for the first time, despite having had limited sleep, no C.V. or any work experience to go on. He was finally being faced with reality and it felt like he was cruelly outmatched.

He felt too embarrassed and deflated to come home to his father and tell him what had happened, as he would have only told him that he brought it on himself for lying around playing video games for too long. However true this was, it didn't make the predicament he was in now any easier.

He screwed up the page of jobs in anger and disgust. Unaware of what he was going to do next, he wandered aimlessly towards the town centre. At a loss, he felt almost in a trance as he walked down a side street. He wasn't sure where it led, but at that point he didn't care much. Oblivious to his surroundings, he heard a female voice shout his name.

Turning round he quickly snapped out of his negative trance. Shelly appeared, with newly dyed blue hair, and hugged him.

"You ok? You looked like you were about to kill somebody. It looked like it would have been a crime of passion and rage too, so what's up?" she asked.

Henry usually hid it if he was upset about something and fronted it up as anger; he shared his father's strong sense of pride. However, due to Shelly's perception, knowledge of psychology and empathy, it was hard for him to keep it from her at this moment in time.

"I just haven't slept much and I've had a bad day so far."

Shelly laughed:

"That can all change. You just walked passed a tea shop. Why don't we go in there? I can only imagine how hilarious it will be seeing people's faces when you fall asleep on the super comfy sofa they've got."

Henry smiled and nodded and they made their way back towards the tea shop. It was a strange-looking setting. It didn't surprise Henry he'd walked past it, even if he had been in a trance of rage.

The front of the shop looked like a very small warehouse. However, once you were inside, there was a till with someone to welcome you and a set-up of chairs, tables and a large sofa which overlooked the window to the street. The more of the store you explored, the more you found. There were shelving units packed with sacks of different flavoured tea. In the back area, there was a stair case which led to a balcony overlooking the rest of the shop.

As Henry was taking in the unusual setting, which was pretty bizarre to him, Shelly asked the lady at the counter:

"Audrey, are the toffs' in today?"

The middle-aged bohemian-looking woman standing behind the counter laughed:

"No dear. Who's your friend?"

Shelly's face lit up with her reply:

"Excellent, this is Henry. He's not interested, but I'll bring you more victim's soon."

Winking at Audrey, Shelly gestured if it was alright to go up to the balcony.

Not really listening to Shelly's conversation with Audrey, Henry followed Shelly up the wooden spiral stair case. The upper balcony area had an old style carpet, lamps on side tables next to each armchair and a sofa with a book case fitted in the wall filled with classics. Shelly reassured Henry:

"If you do want to sleep on the sofa, I will keep you safe from the cougar at the front till."

Henry's eyes enlarged with surprise:

"What?!"

Shelly laughed and told Henry how, if there was someone she didn't like trying to force her or one of her friends on a date, she'd sometimes get them drunk and set them up with Audrey for the night as she liked younger men.

"Don't worry if I tell her someone's not interested like I did a minute ago. She leaves them alone. It's like our safe word, if you will."

Henry looked concerned about how formidable this young lady could be. Although it had terrified him to a degree, Shelly's story had woken him up, and her frankness had earned his trust in a weird way. So he told her about his predicament with trying to find work, and how his life had been turned upside-down by his grieving father breaking the internet.

Shelly started to realise how trapped Henry had become over the years, each year he spent in online captivity making it harder and harder to break the cycle and get out of his virtual reality. What made it worse was she could understand how he had come to give up on life and people, as the majority of them had only judged him on his success or lack of at school, or how they thought he should look and behave.

She didn't want to give him an excuse to revert back to his self-pitying and lazy attitude because it would not help him progress. Instead, she invited him to come back to Cone-ee-Island with her.

Henry explained he didn't have any money and that he didn't want to be in debt or keep taking charity.

As she rose from her chair, Shelly smiled as her freshly-dyed sapphire blue hair brought out the excitement in her green eyes.

"What I'm going to give you is far more valuable and dignified than an ice-cream or money."

Henry looked baffled as he followed her out of the shop en route to the ice cream shop.

The two new friends arrived at the stylish ice-cream parlour. The smell of sweetness greeted them as Henry and Shelly walked across the squeaky clean, black and white floor tiles. JJ was behind the counter sweeping the area.

"Jeremy" Shelly called in an annoying manner.

Glowing with embarrassment, (as he hated that name) JJ welcomed his friends.

"Is your Dad in JJ?" Shelly asked, satisfied that the embarrassment she had caused him was enough to deter any time-wasting flirting from her transatlantic admirer.

JJ shuffled out the back to get his father.

Henry briefly took a moment to appreciate the establishment and how much time and effort must have gone into building both the business and the store he found himself in. It had started to remind him of the conversation he and his father had held before. Henry was starting to realise that his father was right. He was standing in a place that people would remember for years in the future. Furthermore, it would be sorely missed if it closed in the future and it would feel as though a sentimental piece of the town had crumbled.

"Are you even listening? He'll be out here in a minute." Shelly said.

Henry's train of thought was derailed as he asked her to repeat herself.

"We're gonna try and get you a job here. Shane doesn't just let anyone sit in and have a free ice cream, so I'm fairly convinced if he knew you needed a job he'd let you work here, but you have to do the talking and ask." Shelly hurriedly whispered.

They both heard Shane's footsteps descending the stairs, and he appeared at the doorway.

"Hey kids, how's it going?"

Before Henry's nerves could set in, he looked Shane straight in the eye and asked:

"Have you got any jobs available here? I haven't got a C.V. but I'd be up for an interview, and I'd really appreciate the job."

Shane smiled and called for JJ to attend the till and get Shelly an ice cream while he talked business with Henry. They went to the back of the restaurant and sat in a booth.

"You've got the job." Shane exclaimed with a smile.

Seeing the look of pleasant surprise on Henry's face encouraged Shane to elaborate.

"C.V.s don't give me a lot of information anyway. As far as an interview goes, you told me everything I needed to know yesterday. Oscar's a good kid, and friends and associates can tell you a lot about a person. And from what I saw, heard and thought of you yesterday, you've got pride.

Lots of JJ's friends from back home in the apple and over here in merry England, have had no money or said they didn't, at least. Not only did you reach in your pocket when I offered you an ice-cream, you also refused when the others offered you money.

Freeloaders are a dime a dozen, and most of them would have written down 'trustworthy' on their resume. You actually proved it yesterday.

Hell, I could be wrong, you could prove me wrong but the second you did you'd be out on your ass. And whatever money or deal you got wouldn't be nearly as valuable as the loyalty, trust and friendship you'd lose. But I'm willing to give you a chance here. I ain't gonna lie to you, son, there's gonna be days when you ain't gonna want to come into work, but I'm hoping for both our sakes you will."

Henry nodded respectfully, acknowledging the candour with which Shane was speaking to him. He then asked

Shane about training. Henry was happy to admit that he had no experience with retail or ice-cream before.

Once again, Shane was impressed and explained:

"We all gotta start somewhere kid. This floor was filthy this morning, now you can see the ceiling in it. Jobs like that have to be done in here. If you're willing to do the work, I'm willing to help. I ain't gonna have you mopping the floor all the time.

There're a lot of jobs to do in here and we change things around all the time. My boy does the books too, sometimes. I'd be happy to show you the ropes of the business somewhere down the line, but the most important thing for now are the little jobs.

I look at certain shops these days and I see dickhead bosses treating their staff like trash. Then their boss comes down and treats them like trash. The only people who profit from that are the fat cat assholes up the chain. Then I see kids like you who have all the potential in the world turn sour because they ain't being treated with respect, and they're not getting taught anything because their dickhead bosses don't know what they're doing either. It's a sorry sight to see, I can tell you that much.

Now I think you're like me in that if someone don't treat you right, you ain't gonna do a damn thing for them; but if someone does treat you right, you'll work hard and put your all into it.

This is an ice cream shop; people don't need ice-cream like they need things at the grocery store. It's a treat, it can be a night out, and it can be a special occasion. If the shop team are happy, then they can make the customers happy too."

The insight and opportunity Shane was offering inspired Henry and he felt positive compared to the negativity he had been feeling earlier. His tiredness had diminished and he felt awake and alert enough to ask Shane what he needed to know about salary and start date. He found out that he would start on minimum wage, but with each new skill and job he did and learned how to do, it would increase by 20p. Once he had learned all the skills, he would be on a very competitive retail salary of £8.80 per hour.

Henry also found out that he would be starting work the following day, which he was more than happy to accept (even though he was expected to show up at 8 o'clock in the morning).

Buzzing with positivity, Henry left the shop. As he walked home in the hot summer sun, he heard the familiar drone of a plane soaring in the sky. He had heard this sound at points all the way through his life but, much like a lot of things in the town; he only really noticed it then.

Passing the tea shop on his way back he noticed an eccentric looking young man in a suit talking to Audrey. He looked quite obnoxious in the way he was pointing at what drink he wanted. Henry chuckled to himself, wondering if the pontificating ponce knew what she might do to him.

Arriving home, Henry called out for his father. After several calls and no response, Henry started to search the house. He wouldn't normally be worried. However, it was just after 12 o'clock on a Monday afternoon. One of the few enjoyments Cliff took in retirement was watching his favourite gardening show Get up off your Grass. Henry began searching the house, fearing for the worst. He'd never seen his father in such a state as he had yesterday. He started to panic that he may have done something terrible. Each empty room he searched upstairs filled him with more panic for what the next may hold.

Making his way back downstairs, Henry went through the living room into the kitchen. Looking through the hatched window at the end of the house, he noticed his father out in the garden, tending to his botanical masterpiece.

Sighing with relief, Henry laughed to himself for being so silly. He went out to the garden to join his father.

"Hello Henry, what have you been doing today?"

His father enquired. Henry's face lit up with achievement; before he even said anything, Cliff knew that his son had met the challenge he had set out for him. Leaving his bulb patch, Cliff walked across the grass to his patio table where a fresh bottle of champagne was waiting for them.

"Something told me you'd pull it out of the bag, old boy." Cliff exclaimed with a smile as he popped the cork, pouring two glasses.

Henry laughed:

"Why the Cham-pagna?"

Cliff laughed "It makes good news taste even better. Now let's hear all about it."

With that, the father and son sat at the patio table enjoying champagne in the sun.

Soaking in the relaxed atmosphere, he appreciated the opportunity to enjoy an afternoon with his father. Henry relayed the story of how the short sighted and tempered manager at Cutting-Craft had almost broken his spirit. Admitting that his lifestyle had put him at a disadvantage in seeking employment in the current work climate, Henry managed to open his father's eyes to how difficult it was to sell yourself for a job and meet the various criteria that modern employers took for granted. In Cliff's day, he didn't need to prepare a C.V., he just asked for work and once he had done enough jobs and learnt enough skills, he never had a problem gaining employment.

Henry then continued to explain how he had come to meet a bunch of new friends the previous night and how he got his foot in the door of the ice cream shop.

Cliff sat back and laughed:

"This town's still got its charm of putting people in the right place at the right time."

Sipping his champagne, he added:

"Although the buildings, fashions and times are different, it's good to see that some things haven't changed. Whatever people say about the town's appearance and reputation, there's a certain magic to it sometimes. Being an out of touch old fart, I'd forgotten about it. Hell I didn't even think I could be surprised anymore. But thanks to you and Fred, I've been rather pleasantly proven wrong."

Henry remembered how his father was missing "get off your grass". In all the years he could remember when his father wasn't working, he'd be watching the sarcastic old geezer who hosted it, pottering around people's gardens and improving them, while giving them a rollicking for neglecting them. At the end of the show the garden would have been transformed into a masterpiece; but Henry always wondered if it was truly worth it as the participants would suffer verbal humiliation on camera.

"How come you haven't got your crappy garden show on today?" Henry asked.

Cliff leaned back with a profound look of realisation on his face. Answering much like his late great friend:

"All the year's I was watching that salty old geezer give people a hard time for neglecting the wonders their garden held, I never took his advice myself. Of course it's easier to have a laugh at someone else's short comings. Fred actually gave me the prompt I needed to renovate the garden and treat it as a project.

He made me come to realise that I missed the obligation of getting up for work. Quite recently he inspired me to enjoy it while I could, so I find myself out here enjoying what I have, rather than watching someone make other people's lives a misery on television for the reward of something they could have enjoyed doing themselves."

Through their exchange of stories and what they had both learned in their respective situations; the father and son found themselves talking and getting to know each other as if they'd just met in a pub and hadn't seen each other for years. It was almost as though their conflicting, yet similar, life styles had kept them distanced from one another for as long as they could remember.

It wasn't spoken out loud, but they both appreciated where fate had taken them on this warm summer's afternoon.

The next morning Henry was wide awake and looking forward to his first day at work. He had his doubts and worries whether he would wake up in time. Luckily the adrenaline and subconscious excitement of what opportunities the new work place offered socially woke him with ease. Dressed in record time, he left for work.

Arriving at the shop perfectly punctual, Henry was greeted by Shane who was reassured by the young man's time-keeping abilities.

"Awesome, you're on time, that's always a great start. Now, first task of the day is cleaning. If you've got any questions, shoot 'em straight at me. It's my shop and I'll respect the fact you wanna learn how I run it, from cleaning to book-keeping, it's all important."

With that Henry, took to cleaning the shop. Trade was very slow at that time in the morning, apart from a few school children coming in for ice creams and drinks. Shane was serving behind the till while Henry mopped the floor.

Some of the children started laughing as a particularly obnoxious child asked why there was a tub of lard in an ice cream shop. Henry overheard the ill-mannered brat's comments. Shane had foreseen this sort of situation arising sooner or later due to Henry's size and the horrible behaviour he'd witnessed in the short time he'd been in Britain. Clocking the culprit and her laughing lackeys, Shane quickly intervened:

"You kids can leave now, and if you ever disrespect any of my members of staff who help provide you with your ice cream, you'll never set foot in my store again! Now go to school and practice being decent."

Taken back by Shane's reprimand, the children apologised taking nothing but a slice of humble pie to school with them as they left the shop. Henry was seething with anger; however, witnessing how Shane had defused the situation with such style had impressed him.

Henry thanked him for sticking up for him and carried on with his cleaning duties.

As Shane wanted Henry to have a good understanding of the jobs required of him and wanted to test his work ethic, he had given him an 11-hour shift with a paid hour-long lunch break (including a free dessert of his choosing). Henry met Shane's expectations and worked as hard as he could. From cleaning the front of house dining areas and washing the pots and plates to learning how to operate the till, Henry wasn't bored for a minute.

Due to the freshness of the job and the starting of a new era in his life, he didn't even once glance at the clock. The songs being played on the old fashioned juke-box at the side of the shop started to imprint on his mind; he would enjoy them for years to come as they would remind him of this fresh start life had offered him.

Towards the end of the shift, Henry had started waiting people's tables. This was a strategy Shane used once the shop got busy, as the customers looking for a quick ice cream to go would be served at the till and the customers who wanted to sit in could relax and decide what they wanted. By this point, JJ and Shane were working the till point because most of the customers were taking their ice cream to go.

Henry took down the customers' orders, giving them a price quote with the calculator Shane had armed him with.

Suddenly, Henry came across a familiarly unfriendly face. It was the belligerent, bolshie shop manager he had met the previous day, and with him was the nasty school girl from earlier in the day. As her overbearing father was there, the girl had a renewed sense of audacity.

Trying to rise above the hostile vibes which were coming from the table, Henry proceeded to welcome them to the store and take their order. Bill scoffed as he put down the menu:

"Well, well, look who it is. I can see you fitting into a place like this. An American ice cream restaurant, yes I think this is much more your thing than my store."

His equally irritating smug daughter sat giggling.

Henry found himself battling with his pride. He had loved his new job up until now, but this man and his daughter were deliberately trying to make his day bad, simply to make theirs better.

Uncharacteristically in a situation like this, Henry took their order and did his best to remain calm.

Shane had noticed the child from earlier and also noticed the body language of her father. Most importantly, however, he had noticed Henry's demeanour and how it had changed since listening to their order. Once Henry went back to the counter, Shane promptly asked for the order sheet for their table.

Making his way to their table, Shane was confronted by Bill:

"What's going on here? We're supposed to be getting ice-cream, not our order back. That fat boy better not have eaten it."

The child laughed even harder than before in adoration of her father's bully boy humour.

Shane calmly silenced the laughter with a piercing look at both parties, before quietly explaining:

"Okay, we can do this two ways. You can apologise to my colleague Henry and stop being offensive. Or you can both leave my store and never come back. The choice is entirely yours, so what's it to be?"

Totally affronted by Shane's ultimatum, Bill shrugged:

"Look I'm Bill McCray the manager of Cutting-Craft. We were only having a joke. Bring Henry the Eighth back over here and we'll have some ice cream. It's my daughter's treat for doing well at school for God's sake."

Taking in the reference to the large historical English king, Shane responded with authority:

"You may be able to treat people how you like in your own store Mr McCray, but I find your attitude and comments offensive and inappropriate for the family environment I've created internationally. As you'll be well aware, the manager of the premises has the right to refuse to serve a customer. I am invoking that right, right now. Please leave."

Gawking in disbelief, Bill rose from his seat, blushing in embarrassment. "Absolute joke this is," he muttered as he took his equally embarrassed daughter home with him.

Shane had managed to exile the toxic manager with minimal fuss.

Once Henry's shift had ended, Shane called him out to the back for a chat.

Standing in the dark creaky wooden corridor, which led to the exterior of the establishment, the two started to chat.

"Thanks for sticking up for me today, I really appreciate it. Normally I would have done something about it but you handled it a lot better than I would have." Henry admitted. Shane explained to his grateful employee:

"I should be thanking you, not only did you acknowledge you didn't know how to handle situations but you made an effort to not to escalate the situation. Plus, you'll learn how to handle dickheads like that. In fact, he was a precise example of what kind of a moron the retail system churns out, like I was telling you about the other day. I don't care if it's a snot nose kid or the goddam president, no one will disrespect my staff, whatever country I'm working in."

Agreeing with his new manager, Henry asked how he had done for his first day.

Shane didn't answer at first but invited Henry to come upstairs and gave him a tour of the rest of the building. There was a small but stylish two bedroomed flat in the upstairs department of the store.

As they got upstairs Shane invited Henry to sit down in

his upstairs kitchen. There was a soothing view of the street below as the night started to close in and the street lights illuminated the road. Pouring his new employee a drink, Shane explained how he had already expanded his business empire through his personally-designed strategy of training people up from scratch and eventually leaving them in charge of the store. So far he had built up around 20 different stores in the states, most of which were very successful, each with a different name to suit the town they were in. Each parlour had had accommodation upstairs where he had lived for a while until his new protégé was ready to take over. At that point, the accommodation was handed over to the manager and he or she would manage the store. Shane would take 45% of the profits from the store, the remaining 55% went to the manager. As this was the first ice cream parlour he had opened in Britain, he had decided to give it the same name as his first one in his home town of Coney Island.

Shane explained that JJ was interested in starting his own business venture with Terry (which Shane respected).

It became apparent to Henry that if he stayed loyal to Shane and continued to work hard and learn under his tutelage, like he did on his first day, he could be next up to manage the store a couple of years down the line. This incentive gave Henry the structured future to work towards which a lot of people could only dream of. It was just up to him to work hard and stay dedicated to the opportunity.

S.A. BALLANTYNE

Sea-Side City

Surveying The Territory

Surveying the Territory

Cover photo sourced from:
Pexels

Ferris Wheel Picture
Originally uploaded by:
Guilherme Rossi

Picture of Female
Originally uploaded by:
Ricardo Mitchel

Cover Design/ Fading by:
S.A. Ballantyne

SURVEYING THE TERRITORY

Sporting effervescent pink hair, and with luminous green eyes, Shelly always stood out from the crowd.

Her clothing style varied depending on the occasion, which currently was rocking casual jeans and a vest top, but she was rarely seen without her wireframe glasses.

Concluding a short, mid-semester weekend break away in Spain, Shelly had returned to the Sea-Side City happy and refreshed. Prior to her holiday, the bright young psychology student had become bored with her surroundings and needed a short getaway to help her resettle.

Upon her return, Shelly was surprised at how happy she felt to be back in the Sea-Side City in which she had started her independent adult life. Her spontaneous trip to Spain had been perfectly timed to break the cycle of her boredom. However, the location she had chosen was remote. Although she had been able to enjoy the beautiful sunrises and sunsets: the one thing she craved more was people.

Shelly's main interest and fascination in life was people and social situations. A passionate psychology student at the City's university, Shelly had an unquenchable thirst for knowledge about how people think and react to different social situations. Though she was a keen student with the potential to make revolutionary discoveries in the field, some would consider her enjoyment of social engineering inappropriate and distasteful.

It was coming toward the latter part of her first year at university and she had just finished attending a lecture. Shelly was eager to use her refreshed state of mind to make new friends.

She'd already got to know the people on her course and she found them to be slightly tedious.

Other than a small group of student friends she'd made at the university, the only local friend she had was Audrey, an eccentric bohemian who owned a tea shop.

Venturing into the town centre with fresh eyes Shelly observed her surroundings. She took a moment to just observe the hustle and bustle of the town, sitting on a bench outside the job centre. The job centre was often an epicentre of human emotions. Some people entering or exiting the building hopeful and joyful about the prospects of employment and opportunity; but most at negative boiling points of sorrow or rage.

To her surprise, the job centre wasn't particularly busy; however, the town-centre was still showing other signs of life. A few characters caught her attention, one of whom was a lad passing by on a bike with an amplifier strapped to his back. It sounded like it was playing an old country and western song. However, she couldn't quite make out the song it was booming out owing to the quality of the sound and the speed at which he was riding.

Shelly chuckled to herself as the reckless rider swerved round the corner, narrowly avoiding another young man. The other young man jumped out of his skin at the high speed, musical hazard.

Once her amusement had passed, Shelly focused on the startled young man more closely.

He stood out due to his pale skin, which suggested he hadn't seen much sunlight.

It was almost indistinguishable from the platinum blonde hair upon his head.

Though he stood out, Shelly couldn't see him too clearly because of the distance between them.

"Shell, you're back!"

Her train of thought was interrupted by the unmistakeable, American accent of her friend Jeremy-Joe

Mahoney. Happy to see her friend, Shelly rose to embrace him:

"Haven't been back long my friend."

Predictably, JJ invited Shelly back to his father's ice-cream shop. The main reason Shelly had left was due to the repetitive cycle her life had become over the previous few months. However, her reflective break had allowed her to realise that her expectations of life and people may have been too high.

With this in mind, Shelly gracefully accepted JJ's invitation.

Upon arriving at the Cone-ee-Island ice-cream parlour, just south of the town centre, Shelly's other friends Terry and Oscar were waiting for them.

Meanwhile back in the town centre, the young man who had been startled by the musical bike rider had shaken off the shock and made his way to the Coastal-Collage shopping centre. After a few minutes of light window shopping, he received an e-mail on his smart phone from his friend Fred Smith. The message read:

"Dear Connor,

I hope this message finds you safe and well, I have enjoyed our outings and hope to meet again soon. Unfortunately, I am feeling unwell today and am unable to see you.

Kind Regards
Fred Smith"

Connor replied, encouraging his friend to get well soon.

Fred and Connor had only met recently, but Fred had become something of a mentor to Connor in just those few short meetings. Following a traumatic experience several years ago, Connor had barely been outside the confines of his house for years, apart from occasions other than being carpooled to work.

In a liberating chain of events, he had decided to change his confined lifestyle and explore his hometown for the first time in years. This chain of events occurred due to his loss of the internet and a nostalgic craving for sour sweets from his childhood. The first few days of his week off had been extremely productive and eye opening. However, this would be the first day he was out without company. Taking the opportunity to improvise, Connor perused the shops.

Back at Cone-ee-Island, Shelly found herself back to the grind with the same group of friends, doing the same thing she had grown weary of before her break.

Her jovial friend Oscar would joke about how fat he'd got since spending so much time at the ice-cream parlour. JJ was forever trying to win her affections and look for activities to do with Shelly away from the group. JJ's best friend and aspiring entrepreneur Terry would be trying to compete for her affections, and banter would ensue.

Although she found it funny at first, had enjoyed spending time with them and liked them all as people, after seven months of the same cycle, in the same locations, Shelly was getting bored. She was partly to blame for the way things had turned out. She would socially manipulate the group for her own entertainment at times and benefit from knowing their personalities as well as she did. But now she was looking to expand her experiences and friends within the Sea-Side City.

Her train of thought was interrupted as the proprietor of the establishment and JJ's father, Shane brought the group their complimentary ice-creams. JJ took the opportunity to try and impress Shelly:

"Welcome back Shelly, yours is on the house!"

Shane noticed his son's sly attempt to charm Shelly at his expense:

"Well they all were Jeremy-Joe, but now they're on you, kiddo."

Terry started sniggering at his mate's social failure:

"Thanks mate, you're a real philanthropist."

Embarrassed at his father's interjection and irritated at

his friend's satire, JJ flicked a small portion of ice-cream at Terry, exclaiming:

"It's on him too!"

Oscar predictably joked:

"Ooh, creamed him."

Outraged at his son's juvenile behaviour, Shane raised his voice:

"Hey! Will you knock that off? What do you think this is, kindergarten?"

Somewhat amused at the outburst, Shelly laughed with her friends. But once she'd finished her ice-cream she excused herself from the group and returned to town.

Enjoying the warmth that the sun offered, but finding it difficult to see from the glare of its rays, she headed to the Coastal-Collage shopping centre to buy a hat.

On her travels she spotted Connor, the pale lad she had seen earlier from afar. He was sitting on a bench with a bag of sweets, just watching the world go by.

Something about him made her want to get to know him. Distracted from her objective of buying a hat, she decided to go and introduce herself, in classic Shelly fashion.

Blissfully unaware he was being watched, Connor was enjoying the nostalgic flavours of his childhood, enjoying just watching the world go by as the atmospheric chatter of shoppers echoed around the Coastal Collage shopping centre. He had recently taken up people-watching on the advice of Fred Smith.

Shelly approached him, asking if she could have one of his sweets. Connor was happy to share them with her. Encouraged by his friendly behaviour, she asked if she could join him. Delighted at the prospect of making another friend, Connor welcomed her.

Shelly started the conversation, referring to the encounter with the bike earlier, enquiring if Connor was alright.

Thankful for her concern, Connor admitted that it had startled him momentarily. He started to open up to her about how he had only just started going out again after years of living in fear.

"What brought that on?"

Shelly asked, knowing that agoraphobic tendencies were often developed as a result of a traumatic incident.

After years of barely talking to anyone about his troubles and only just coming to terms with them, Connor started to divulge the burdens of his soul.

"It all started when I was in secondary school. I'd been trying to study so much to get good grades. My parents were ashamed of me because all the way through school I'd been gradually moved down the sets. I hadn't been taught anything and the lower the sets got the harder it was to learn because of the people in there.

Anyway, so I'm studying and I'm being convinced that if I don't get these grades and I don't get A-Cs my life's not going to be worth living. So basically I'm stressed beyond belief.

One day on my way home after school, I end up being shoved by a guy from Jack's-Ville.

Because I'm so stressed I shoved him back. Before I know it there were five of them beating me to unconsciousness.

I'm not a fighter, I never have been, but after that I never wanted to go out again. I flunked all of my exams; my parents were mortified. They moved up to Congleton for work, but they made it clear they didn't want me to go with them. Eventually I ended up staying in a hostel until I qualified for a council flat. I've been working for a catering company since I left, the work gets me out of the city, and thanks to the progress of the internet, since moving into my council flat I haven't had to leave my house or see any of them again."

Shelly found herself fascinated at Connor's story. During her eight months at university in the Sea-Side City, she had only seemed to experience her fellow students trying to cover up their insecurities with bravado and superficial fronts. It was one of the first times she'd seen someone of his age be that honest.

Connor felt drained having offloaded his painful history to a complete stranger. After a couple of moments of reflective silence, he added:

"Sorry, you probably didn't want to know all that. That's the second time this week I've blurted that out. My Mum and Dad were right all along. I really need to get over this. I mean it was five years ago."

Shelly interjected:

"It doesn't matter how long you hold stuff like that in for, it will come out! Didn't you have anyone to talk to about it? How did you manage to avoid everyone at youth housing?"

Connor chuckled:

"As scary as that place was, no one was up at seven in the morning and the shop down the road was open. I didn't have many friends at school, just the alternative kids, but I drifted away from them anyways. It's a pretty scary place to be in life when you're afraid of anyone wearing a tracksuit."

Shelly started to realise the overwhelming fear Connor had been living with, and the effects it had taken on everything in his life. Not only was she pleasantly surprised by his honesty, Shelly wanted to use her knowledge, recourses and understanding to help her troubled new friend get his life back on track.

"So what's the plan?"

she asked.

Unsure, Conner shrugged his shoulders and explained:

"Use my time off work and see how it goes, I guess. At the beginning of the week I booked my first week off work and just went out to see if they still sold these sour sweets. Then I got talking to this old guy and I just started talking and I've been out ever since.

He suggested going to a different area of the town each day, we only got through one so far though. In all honesty, I don't really know where I'm going from here though."

Recognising similarities in their polar opposite lifestyles and an opportunity for positive change, Shelly approved of exploring the town and suggested they met up the next day to go round it together. They agreed to meet at the same bench, before parting ways for the day. Looking back at Connor as she left to return home and catch up on her studies, Shelly smiled to herself feeling positive vibes about the prospects of her new friendship.

Though he hadn't moved from his bench, Connor felt similarly contented with how his week was turning out. Sad as his friendless lifestyle of isolation had seemed, Connor was starting to appreciate the new friendships he had formed.

The following day, the two new acquaintances reunited at the bench. Both punctual on their arrival, Shelly and Connor quickly made plans to explore Penelope Park. It was a short walk away from the town centre, presenting a harmonious setting for the two new friends to get to know one another.

Entering the park, they were greeted by the relaxing rustling of trees blowing in the wind.

Having been absent from the park for several years, it wasn't long before Connor's attention was drawn to a number of people congregated at the opposite side of the park.

It was difficult for Connor to make them out; however, they all appeared to have long hair and were wearing ancient battle clothing.

Shelly had anticipated they may cause him concern and reassured him:

"Don't worry about them, they're the Sea-Side Saxons. If anything, they'll protect you from any danger while you're here."

Increasingly more confused as to why a park in 21st

century Britain was being occupied by people dressed like Anglo-Saxons, Connor asked:

"The Sea-Side Saxons? Who are they and what are they doing here?"

Shelly chuckled, imitating a voiceover from a wildlife documentary:

"Ah, the Saxons… fascinating creatures; people from all walks of life, coming together as sworn guardians of Penelope Park. They will break up any fight, they will apprehend any criminal: all for the noble cause of creating a safe place for people of all ages to relax and enjoy the tranquillity of Penelope Park."

Both laughing at the comedy value of Shelly's narrative on the Saxons, they further observed them from afar. There must have been around 40 of them, though the numbers varied from day to day due to their respective jobs and commitments. A group of seven were sitting in a circle playing customised ancient instruments, with a couple of them telling children stories.

Around 15 of them were practising combat with ancient weaponry and shields, one of whom was an imposing female warrior with striking red hair, wielding a large staff, besting all in her way. The friendly exhibition was entertaining passers-by and tourists of all ages.

The other 18 were scattered in small groups around the park, serving as watchmen and women, chatting to inquisitive passers-by.

Connor was amazed at how much his hometown had changed in his six years of cyber-hibernation. Shelly, amused at his bemusement, encouraged him with:

"Come on, let's make some new friends."

With that, they went and chatted to one of the watchmen. He was an older man of around 50 with a bushy grey beard. Wearing a classic woollen hip-length undershirt with a fur pelt covering his shoulders, the seasoned watchman sat on a wooden stool with a spear in his left hand.

Greeting her with the Sea-Side Saxon's signature forearm grasping handshake, the seasoned elder introduced himself as Wade, named after the Anglo Saxon god of the sea.

Connor remained respectfully quiet, only answering when addressed by the man. He was still quite overwhelmed by the Saxons being in the park, and didn't have the confidence to fully converse with Wade.

Shelly, on the other hand, couldn't wait to talk to a representative of this unusual tribe of warriors

"Who's that red headed girl thrashing everyone with the staff over there?"

Wade informed them with authority:

"That there is Boudica, the finest stick fighter and grappler we have. She's been following our ranks since she was a girl of 14. She also takes part in local professional wrestling shows."

Shelly asked:

"Aren't those pre-determined though?"

Wade cleared his throat

"You're welcome to go and discuss that with her. I doubt you'll be seeing anyone best her in a combat situation, rigged or otherwise."

As Shelly and Wade's conversation continued, Connor remained silent. He was constantly scanning the area for his own peace of mind. While she gained information regarding the history of the Penelope Park Saxons regiment, Shelly was also observing Connor's nervous behaviour in an impressive display of multitasking.

It had become apparent he was becoming uncomfortable.

Shelly had refrained from conducting a social experiment on him the first time they had met; however, now the opportunity had presented itself, she couldn't resist.

Though she could tell by his body language he was uncomfortable, his frantic head movements made it difficult for her to see his face.

Suddenly, as his head turned back, their eyes met. She now saw the haunting pain behind his eyes. In all of her past experiences, she had never felt such an immediate strong empathic connection.

Her previous social experiments had usually been satisfying; this was mainly because she conducted them on people with superiority complexes or who pretended to be something they weren't. She'd even occasionally managed to help some people learn about themselves.

However, she quickly decided to move on and allay Connor's increasing fear.

Excusing themselves from Wade's company, they made their way to a nearby bench.

"How are you feeling?"

Shelly asked, genuinely concerned for her troubled friend. Connor sighed:

"I don't know to be honest. It's surreal how much everything's changed. I've been cooped up for almost six years. Now everything's just different. If I go back to the way things were, just living on the internet and working, I'll always know that there's more out there to see and do. But at the same time, I've still got this fear in this place. There are too many people around here, I feel like a sitting duck."

Shelly placed her hand over his. Connor's uncomfortable, introverted body language started to open up and ease. He hadn't experienced a compassionate interaction since early childhood. He didn't quite know how to react. Such a chain of events would be quite unremarkable to the average person. However, the rush of emotions and supressed memories overwhelmed Connor, causing him to break down. He felt too drained to be embarrassed, though he had no reason to be, as he was finally addressing the issues which had been negatively affecting his life for years.

Shelly held him under her denim jacket, concealing his

tears from the rest of the people in the park, reassuring him:

"Take all the time you need, no one can see you. They're all just interested in their own lives. You're safe with me."

Anonymous to the surrounding public in the shelter of her arms, Connor felt safe.

The scent of her perfume, strawberries and vanilla, became stronger as he nuzzled into her chest; the fragrance soothed him and took his mind back to memories of childhood sweets.

After a few short moments (which felt like an eternity to Connor), he had managed to subdue the tears. They shared a couple of laughs. To hide the evidence of tears in his eyes, Connor put on a pair of sunglasses he had folded over his collar.

Shelly enquired as to how long it had been since Connor had been in Penelope Park.

Connor took a second to collect his thoughts; it had been over seven years since the 22 year old had ventured into Penelope Park.

He started to recall his last experiences. Connor was friends with the alternative kids at his school. They used to listen to various forms of rock music and dress in an alternate style to the other youths at the school.

Suddenly, Connor came to a realisation:

"They claimed to be different and accepting, listening to music which empathised with being judged and overcoming judgement.

But from what I remember they were more judgemental than half the bullies in the school. Always judging me for not liking the right bands or not liking the same things they did!"

Shelly started to suspect that Connor may have had some underlying anger towards the park which he may have overlooked due to the initial trauma which had caused his life of confinement. Whatever it was, she could fully relate to what he was saying.

In her experience, those who had been bullied often turned into passive aggressive bullies themselves, and the music targeted at teenagers would encourage this behaviour by showcasing the frustrations of a generation. Taking her revelation into consideration, she went on to reassure Connor:

"The best way to lay bad memories to rest is to create positive new ones."

With this in mind, they made a joint decision to go for a walk in the park each day they met up.

After exchanging phone numbers and meeting up a few more times in the park over the course of the week, Shelly started to notice Connor's confidence was building. She took great pride in this as her influence on his life had played a great part in this improvement. Much to Connor's delight, his boss had allowed him to extend his time off from a week to two. Since they had conquered the park together and the afternoon turned to evening, Shelly suggested they go for an ice-cream to celebrate.

Shelly and Conner arrived at Cone-ee-Island, to find Terry, JJ and Oscar already there. Shelly had anticipated this and had an ulterior motive, i.e. for Connor to meet her friends.

She wanted Connor to make more friends and gain more experience in social situations.

However, it wasn't long before she realised that a small group of males, predominantly competing to court her, wasn't the best environment to introduce him to.

Oscar welcomed Connor and made an effort to get to know him.

JJ and Terry on the other hand, were not as welcoming. Just as Connor started to open up to Oscar, Terry interrupted:

"So you've done nothing but catering for six years? You're joking. Shelly, where did you find this guy?"

JJ chuckled, feigning an apology by laughing.

Connor didn't really know what to say and was visibly uncomfortable with the rugged banter. Shelly found herself disgusted with her friends' passive-aggressive degenerate behaviour. In a moment of anger, she snapped:

"You know Terry; if you weren't so good at ripping people off you wouldn't be able to do anything with your useless sociology course, so don't look down on Connor for actually holding down a job!"

while getting up from her seat and encouraging Connor to leave with her.

Oscar's face dropped:

"I guess that's put me 'something' out of luck too then."

Shelly felt her stomach drop as she and Connor left. In her outburst of rage, she had inadvertently offended Oscar who was on the same course. Angry at Terry, JJ and herself, she had no idea how she could have made such a careless remark.

Usually in social situations of that nature, Shelly had an advantage because she didn't feel emotionally invested. On this occasion however, she felt an overwhelming sense of protectiveness towards Connor.

After a few moments of silent reflection as they walked down the street, Shelly realised how her emotions had affected her judgement.

As Shelly processed the events in her head, Connor felt awkward walking in such tense silence. In an effort to start another conversation, he gasped:

"I'm sorry; I didn't mean to embarrass you in front of your friends."

Still angry, Shelly ranted:

"It's not your fault. They're all so boring! Oscar just sits their making crass jokes and the other two imbeciles act like a pair of schoolboys. I've been having such a good time with you these last few days. Why did I have to ruin it by taking you there? They're always in there!"

Connor wanted to help, but he felt at a loss for words.

He awkwardly patted her on the back. Though he didn't have the confidence to look at her while doing it, Shelly smiled at his inexperienced attempt at affection. As they continued walking, she took his hand.

Connor's pale face quickly transformed into a warm shade of pink as they walked off into the evening, hand in hand.

"So where do you want to go now?"

Connor asked.

Calmed of her irritation, Shelly giggled:

"Fancy a cuppa?"

Though he didn't know where this would be taking place, Connor accepted the offer.

The sky had blossomed into an unusual blend of purple and orange as the sun had set.

Concluding a short walk from the ice cream parlour to the tea room, Shelly introduced Connor to her friend Audrey.

"Hello Shelly, how wonderful to see you again, who's this nice young man?"

The eccentric old bohemian spinster behind the counter welcomed Shelly.

Shelly replied:

"His name's Connor and he's mine."

The three of them chuckled; Audrey then prompted:

"Well, in that case, you two better take the balcony before the toffs get here."

Shelly took Connor by the hand once again and led him up the wooden spiral stair case to the upper balcony which oversaw the lower floor of the shop.

At the top of the staircase, a quaint and civilised atmosphere awaited them. Enjoying the pleasant aroma of various herbal teas paired with freshly varnished mahogany; Connor's eyes were drawn to the luxurious leather sofas and dimmed lamps surrounding the table.

Taking their seat, Connor learnt that this section of the tea room was usually reserved for the higher paying customers. Shelly elaborated:

"Normally, the big money toffs from out of town come up here. Or even worse, their kids. Gosh, they're obnoxious!"

Shortly later Audrey came up and brought them their teas. The two young friends were enjoying the romantic atmosphere the venue provided.

After a relaxing chat, they finished their tea. Shelly was at the point of discussing the prospect of a relationship between them when suddenly the front door was barged open.

It was Isaac Bebbington, one of the higher paying customers Shelly had described earlier.

"Table for one please, my bloody friends have stood me up. Oh, and can you move the riff-raff from my balcony as well."

Isaac slurred.

Shelly's face glowed with anger. Quietly seething, she assessed the situation; smiling to herself, she asked Connor:

"Do you want to go for a walk down to the seafront?"

Connor agreed and they promptly left as master Bebbington stumbled up the stairs in a drunken stupor. Feigning a refined voice, Shelly exclaimed:

"Excuse us sir."

Oblivious to the mockery, Isaac mumbled:

"It's quite alright girl."

On their way out, Shelly whispered something in Audrey's ear, before chuckling and joining Connor outside.

"What are you so happy about?"

Connor asked, puzzled at Shelly's amusement and yet more confused as Audrey ran to the door and put a sign up saying the shop was closed.

Shelly told Connor she'd tell him later as she winked at Audrey before they wandered down the street, hand in hand once again, and headed down to the seafront.

Walking down the street, Connor enquired:

"What was going on back at the tea room?"

Shelly started to giggle again:

"I trust you won't tell anyone. Audrey is a complex lady who's lived a very interesting life. She used to work as a prostitute and she's learnt quite a few tricks of the trade. She has a fondness for younger men as they remind her of her youth. As it happens, dear Isaac Babington has a few mummy issues and daddy's pretty rich, so she's going to try her luck with him tonight."

Connor was somewhat shocked,

"No offence to her, but surely he wouldn't be interested."

Shelly sniggered:

"Maybe not, but he was half in the bag when he got there and being an experienced lady of the night, she does have her ways to keep the young men coming back."

They both laughed, finding the situation highly amusing.

Once they had passed the area of suburban housing, they reached their destination. The slightly cooler wind of the sea softly caressed their faces. The sun had slowly set and the esplanade lights colourfully illuminated the pathway to the funfair. It wasn't long into their soulful seaside stroll that the romantic atmosphere was recaptured, and Shelly breached the topic of a potential relationship once again.

They were both feeling butterflies, something Connor had never experienced before. His emotions and nerves caused him to blush and change the subject. Although he wanted to take their relationship beyond friendship; he was afraid that he might do or say something wrong and ruin it. He would rather not have said anything than have said something he wished he hadn't.

From a psychological standpoint, Shelly was more than capable of understanding his evasive behaviour.

However, because she was emotionally invested in the

situation, she wanted more from him. There were a few moments of awkward silence while she formed a plan in her head.

Shelly found herself attracted to Connor due to his uniqueness compared to everyone else she'd met during her time in the Sea-Side City. Not only was he genuine and honest, but he made her feel like she made a difference. Within a few days in her company, Connor was becoming happier and more confident in his surroundings, and had made considerable progress in addressing the problems which had caused him to live such a reclusive life.

What Shelly was unable to take into account was the unresolved emotional baggage that she was carrying. During her years of studying psychology, she had been forever analysing other people's behaviour and looking for various behavioural patterns. However, she had never taken into account the traits in her own behaviour.

Although she had a lot more social and life experience than Connor, Shelly had reserved herself. So fixated was she on trying to be emotionally disengaged and wishing to observe others with emotional anonymity that she had never been in a position to suffer rejection.

Forever standing out in a crowd with her vibrant hair colouring and outlandish personality, she was always attracting the attention of others. However, no matter what her potential suitors like JJ, Terry or countless others had tried to do, she had always managed to remain emotionally detached. But now she was engaged and attracted to someone, she too was feeling the pressure and a fear of rejection.

With these unrecognised feelings simmering below the surface and her judgement clouded by her psychological egotism, Shelly tried to form a plan which would put Connor's feelings to the test, and give him the confidence to pursue what mattered to him in life, all in one night.

"Anyway, shall we go and explore a new area?"

Shelly asked, with a route already planned out in her

head.

Unaware of his companion's underlying agenda, Connor accepted and they continued walking along the esplanade approaching the funfair.

As the sky got darker, the colourful and pleasant atmosphere of the fair became more visible, presenting a soul-warming sight.

The Ferris wheel flashed with the colours of the rainbow and the various food stalls gave off their aromas of candy floss, ice-cream and other seaside delicacies The noise and music from the arcades which surrounded the fair hadn't changed in years. With each of his senses being nostalgically stimulated, Connor was taken back to his childhood, before his traumas and worries of later life. He started to feel safer and more relaxed.

Due to his silent reflection on the safety he was experiencing, he was oblivious to Shelly's uncharacteristic feelings of erratic insecurity.

Though she had made Connor feel safe and secure through leading him through his childhood memories, the destination they were heading for was a dangerous contrast to the pleasures of the funfair.

Before her short break in Spain, Shelly had become bored with the places students normally frequented. She found places like Cone-ee-Island and the family-friendly fair tedious.

She wanted to explore some of the more notorious areas of the town, which had led her to wonder about South Town Harbour.

The abandoned and derelict docks of South Town Harbour had been closed to the public for about three years. Its closure and abandonment had made it a safe haven for criminal activity, and the majority of the town's unsavoury characters.

Shelly's master plan was to take Connor to the harbour. In her mind, this would not only give her a chance to explore the area, but also to build her new suitor's confidence by showing him that he could overcome his fear in even the most notorious of areas.

In addition to her plan being emotionally flawed, Shelly had never before experienced true criminal activity first hand. Having been raised in a decent neighbourhood with low rates of crime; like so many other sheltered middle-class youths, she had become further desensitised to the dangers of criminal activity through films and her scepticism of the media.

This was all about to change; with each step they took, they drew further from the safety and laughter of the funfair and nearer to the darker, grimier depths of South Town Harbour. Connor was so divorced from reality and the media that he wasn't aware how the once peaceful shipping port had slowly regressed into the notorious, crime-filled wasteland South Town Harbour had become.

Walking up the dimly-lit, dirty street, Connor started to notice graffiti along the building walls. Though the street was quiet, the infrequent passers-by stared and glared at the pair of obvious outsiders. Shelly's determination to help Connor, paired with her psychological research of combating intimidation, filled her with false confidence as she whispered to Connor:

"Look straight ahead and don't even acknowledge them."

By this point, the darkness of night had dawn in and Connor had started to realise they had ventured into the wrong side of town. The security he felt at the fair was a distant memory once again.

A dirty-looking tramp dressed in combats and a hooded figure in a large jacket peered over at them ominously from the other side of the street as they reached a pub called The Rough Tide.

Across the road from the pub lay the South Town Harbour docks, sealed off with a 12-foot wall and a couple of construction fences, secured by concrete blocks. Between the construction fences, there was a cracked sign warning the public to keep out. While Connor read the sign and assessed the danger he was in, Shelly noticed an entry point where the fence had been warped out of shape. Shelly tempted Connor, whispering in his ear:

"Come on, how bad can it be? This is supposed to be the worst part of the town. If you can handle this, you can handle anything."

Connor was about to admit he couldn't handle it, but before he could finish his sentence, Shelly had brushed his lips with a brief kiss.

"Come and get me."

She giggled as she rushed across the road through the hole in the fence. Connor was conflicted: his overwhelming fear was demanding he leave, yet his feelings for Shelly and the recent changes he had made in his life empowered him with the courage to pursue her. Primarily, he wanted to get her out of there and ensure her safety.

Sighing with concern, Connor lifted the warped fencing and awkwardly ducked under it, entering the premises.

Scanning the unfamiliar area, his eyes were drawn to a flame-filled barrel, the only source of light in the area. Connor's attention was drawn to a large pile of fly-tipped rubbish, including a bathtub and a range of broken machinery.

A dark old brick building stood to Connor's right. As far as he could see, the vicinity was empty. However, the dried blood stains around the area, paired with the stink of urine suggested that the vicinity was not entirely unoccupied.

"Boo!"

Shelly playfully pounced on Connor from the shadowed corner of the building. Seeing Connor was both startled and irritated, she hugged him adding:

"I'm glad you came."

Accepting her embrace and holding her tight Connor said:

"Can we go now? This place really doesn't look safe and I for one much preferred it at the funfair."

Shelly explained how she was bored with the rest of the city's repetitive and limited forms of entertainment and wanted to explore different areas. She further appealed:

"It'll be good for you to see that the world isn't as bad as you think it is. Plus, I'll owe you one, and I've never owed anyone anything before."

Suddenly their conversation was interrupted by a raucous cheer as the doors of the abandoned building creaked open.

Before they had time to react, a dirty looking young thug jumped out from a broken window concealed in the shadows. He pushed them forward as a dozen people poured out through the creaky wooden doors of the building, circling the dimly flame-lit area.

In amongst the noise from the rabble, Connor heard a distinctive metallic ping.

Following the crowd, a scraggy middle-aged man with a cane hobbled into the middle of the circle. Despite the lack of light, the man was distinctive due to his posture and clothing. Dressed in a worn and weathered mint green coat, his face was dirty, one eye covered by a plastic eye-patch. His cane was also unusual because of its red and white diagonal striping, resembling a candy cane. He cackled, revealing his rotting teeth. Clapping slowly, he cheered:

"Well done son, it looks like you've pulled. Unfortunately, you've done it on my turf. My name is Candy-Shilling."

Shelly, trying to be brave, sniggered:

"I bet that's not on your birth certificate."

Candy-Shilling, his anger erupting, banged his cane on the ground:

"Do you know why they call me that? Because I provide the candy, if you supply the coin; now if you two aren't here to buy, then you're here to work! Seeing as you're so intent on exploring our business complex, why don't me and the lads show you round?

We've got a fight ring round the corner; this scrawny bugger can try his luck against one of mine, and you can keep me entertained love."

Connor's face was traumatised in terror at Candy-Shilling's chilling proposal.

As the crowd of rough and ready thugs sneered and laughed, the barrel of flames started to pop and flare.

BANG!

The fire belched ten foot in the air, letting off a loud report. The explosion startled everyone. During the distraction, the thug behind them had been incapacitated.

Suddenly, Shelly and Connor were grabbed from behind:

"You two, get your arses out now!"

It was the tramp they had seen earlier. He quickly ushered them out, while the other's investigated the explosion.

Once they had escaped through the fence, their unlikely rescuer ignited a small fire, blocking the exit.

"It won't take them long to put that out. Keep moving,"

he exclaimed, hurrying them down the street. The hooded figure who had been accompanying the tramp jumped from the roof of the building down onto the wall, then down to the pavement to join them.

"Good throw mate,"

the tramp chuckled as the four of them ran down the street. Shelly asked:

"Was that you who made that barrel blow up?"

Charles chuckled:

"Usually I wouldn't admit to arson, but no one really gives a toss about anything that happens in that wasteland. My hooded friend here unloaded three-quarters of a can of deodorant by the exit so I could seal it off. We saw you two prats go in, so we knew you'd need rescuing pretty soon. So he lobbed the rest of the can into the fire. I'm just happy they didn't drag you in further, or nearer the barrel, for that matter."

Eventually they reached the safety of the fair. Connor was in shock, but Shelly was curious to know more about their saviours.

"Who are you guys?"
she asked.

The hooded figure removed his hood, revealing himself to be a young man around Shelly's age with short brown hair and blue eyes

"My name's Alex, he's Charles and we're part of the Night Coat program."

The tramp rolled his eyes.

"I guess this is becoming a habit for young Alex over here after last night's little performance. Discretion's clearly not his strong point; I'll never know why he just introduced himself. Anyway, I trust you won't tell anyone else under the circumstances. I'm glad we intervened tonight though. It might not have been the best of nights for you otherwise."

Shelly questioned in confusion:
"Night Coat program?"
Alex refused to elaborate:
"Well, that's another story."
Charles laughed:
"It was a journey through the heartbreak of lost hope."
Irritated at Charles's mirth, Alex changed the subject:
"Anyway, we're going to be off. We don't spend much time around South Town Harbour and the police don't usually go anywhere near it so you probably shouldn't go back."

Charles observed Connor's haunted face:
"Poor lad's in shock, get him a cup of sweet tea would you? And please don't report us to the Old Bill, I wasn't expecting this plum to introduce us by name and show you his gormless mug."

Shelly and Connor nodded in an unspoken agreement of secrecy.

With that, the unlikely pair of local heroes took their leave, ensuring Shelly and Connor made it back to the safety of the fairground.

Once Alex and Charles had gone, Shelly and Connor were left in an awkward silence for several minutes.

Connor was trying to come to terms with what had happened to them in such a brief period of time at South Town Harbour. Meanwhile Shelly's head was divided between feelings of guilt and trying to comprehend the danger she had got them into.

Finally, Shelly realised she needed to apologise.

"I'm so sorry; I should have never dragged you in there. Shall we get that cup of tea?"

Paler than usual and still traumatised, Connor replied:

"You didn't, I followed you. I like you Shelly, but I just can't deal with stuff like this. I'm going to get an early night."

With that Connor left, shaken and vulnerable once more, getting a ranked taxi situated nearby.

Shelly tried to conceal the tears from her eyes. After all her years of hiding in amongst people and trying to protect herself from negative emotions, she had finally been hurt. What made it worse was that deep down she knew it was of her own doing. During her past week with Connor, she had felt more appreciated and engaged than she had done for years. Pulling herself together, Shelly walked back to her halls of residence.

Meanwhile, around the town centre, having paid an extortionate cab fare, Connor arrived back at the safe confines of his flat. As he approached the front door, he noticed a paper slide across the street with the wind. Fred Smith's picture was featured on one of the pages. Connor picked up the paper to investigate.

It was the obituaries section: Fred he had passed away a couple of nights before.

Connor took the paper indoors with him, and was then hit with an outpouring of tears. After experiencing and enduring a highly emotional turn of events in the space of an hour, Connor was exhausted. Once inside his flat, Connor immediately went and threw himself on his bed to grieve the loss of his friend. After everything that had occurred that night, Connor would have appreciated being able to talk to Fred. During the few days that Connor had known Fred, he had come to realise that Fred had had a wealth of life experience which contributed to his calming influence. Connor came to wonder if Fred had ever had any encounters at South Town Harbour, or encounters with Candy-Shilling.

Gazing into the distance, pondering all the unanswered questions, he stared at his extensive collection of DVDs, video games and action figures on display, all of which had been purchased over his years of solitude.

Fred's words rang in his mind:

"You'll always get more out of these things if you have people to share them with."

Connor contemplated the drastic changes his life had undergone. He acknowledged that the majority of them were good and his life felt a lot better. But it was easier to appreciate them from the comfort and security of his home.

Back on the south side of town, Shelly was sitting on her bed in her cramped room at the halls of residence. Perched at the end of her bed, she sipped a hot cup of tea, the window standing open. She stared blankly into the night sky, admiring the crescent moon as purple clouds shifted by.

Although she was sitting in silence, there was an unusual vibrating sound which occurred every now and again, appearing to come through the wall. Her mind was split between the random vibrations and a '70s rock song she had heard on the plane coming home which kept repeating in her head.

Since her return, she had managed to alienate most of her friends and a brand new one within a week. Rocking back and forth in uncomfortable concentration, Shelly reflected on how she had emotionally injured Connor and how she may not see him again. However, she realised that it may not be too late to make amends between her and her other friends back at Cone-ee-Island. Although she had previously found their company tedious, it was far better than the aching guilt-ridden loneliness she currently felt.

Locked in a state of guilt, Shelly remained in her trance for the rest of the evening. Before she eventually drifted off to sleep in the early hours of the morning, she promised herself she would apologise to her group of friends.

Morning broke, bringing new opportunities for both parties to ensure that they had a better day.

Shelly awoke at 11:00, with the hope of going to the library to do some research. Dragging herself out of bed, she threw together an outfit consisting of a summer dress and a denim jacket.

Grabbing some food on the way, she managed to get to the library relatively promptly.

However, her thoughts were continuously drawn back to events from the previous evening.

Unable to get the most out of her allocated study time, Shelly decided to alleviate some of the heavy issues weighing on her conscience.

Immediately after completing the brief notes she had managed to write, she went to the ice-cream parlour to see her friends. On her arrival, Shelly was surprised to see that none of her friends were there.

"Hey there Shelly, how are you doing?"

Shane's voice greeted her from behind the counter.

Shelly turned to face him, asking:

"Where is everyone?"

Surprised, Shane had never seen Shelly this panicked

before. In a calming voice, he counselled:

"I haven't seen any of them yet. JJ and Terry are doing the town. I'm not sure about Oz, though. Why don't you call them? Or if you want to just hang in here you're always welcome. Business is probably going to pick up soon."

Shelly took a moment to consider her options. She didn't often use her phone. She detested how much people relied on them, especially in awkward social situations to save themselves. She also wanted to face her friends in person. However, in this situation, she realised it was necessary to send out a message.

Sending texts to each of her friends in the group, she asked them to meet her in the town centre. To her delight, she received texts back from all of them, confirming they'd be there within the hour.

Not long after, Shelly met her friends in the town centre. Terry and JJ arrived first, shortly after followed by Oscar. Though her friends were still surprised by her outburst the previous day, they were happy to meet up with her.

Shelly apologised to Oscar for her ill-thought out, off-handed comment about his course, which had so offended him.

Being a kind-hearted and forgiving young man, Oscar accepted her apology immediately.

Shelly then took the opportunity to explain to the group why she had been so protective of Connor:

"He suffered a traumatic attack a few years back. He was living a reclusive lifestyle and he's only just started to get the confidence to start trying to combat it. So that's why I was quite protective of him. I don't know if I'll be seeing him again though."

To her surprise, Terry apologised for his behaviour. He thought it was his comments which had caused them to part ways.

Shelly admitted that she had taken him to the wrong

part of town.

"You took a recluse, with low confidence, to South Town Harbour?"

Oscar questioned in dumbfounded amazement.

Shelly was embarrassed to admit her cavalier error of judgement. Terry started to crack up with laughter:

"I'm sorry, that's just too funny."

He gasped for air as his contagious laugh infected the rest of the group one by one. Laughing off their worries as a collective group once again, they returned to Cone-ee-Island.

Her feelings of loneliness the previous night had made Shelly start to appreciate her friends more.

Grateful to have made amends and reunited with her parlour posse, Shelly spent the afternoon laughing and catching up with them.

Later that afternoon they were joined by one of Oscar's old school friends Henry, who had just entered the parlour by chance and out of curiosity.

In contrast, back at Connor's flat, there was a more sombre and fear-stricken atmosphere. Although his eyes could see the same beautiful day as Shelly, his overwhelming fear prevented him from capturing the opportunities it offered.

Connor's mind was haunted with memories of Candy-Shilling and the unknown horrors lurking in the depths of South Town Harbour.

Regardless of how far he was from the danger, Connor's imagination was filling him with panic-invoking scenarios. Paranoid that the people from the harbour were after him, he would likely stay in his room for the remainder of his time off from work. No matter what video games or DVDs he played, his thoughts were never far from darkness.

The following day, Shelly awoke at 7 o'clock, which was unheard of for most students. She felt a change had occurred in her life and wanted to express it in a creative way. Using her burst of energy and early start to her advantage, she decided to dye her hair a different colour. Opening her cramped washroom drawer, she browsed her selection of pre-purchased shades. She decided to use sapphire blue. After two hours her hair was dried and her mind was firmly focused on studying once more. She then made her way back to the library.

She strolled past the tea room en route. To her surprise, she spotted Oscar's friend Henry walking down an adjacent side street.

Though his back was turned, his body language suggested he was angry. Henry was a large lad, and his ire was visible in the way he stomped along the street, resembling a disgruntled caveman.

She called out to him, and eventually got to the bottom of his anger over a cup of tea at Audrey's.

Shelly discovered Henry was looking for a job. After listening to his story, she started to empathise with his situation. It was incredibly difficult to get a job, especially with the disadvantages he had in such a competitive and financially unstable time. Shelly ended up being sidetracked from her objective of studying once again, and dedicated the afternoon to assisting Henry in gaining employment.

Meanwhile, Connor was having a slightly more proactive day than the previous one, having arranged for someone to come round and fix his internet. Though he was still sick with worry, his internet was up and running within an hour. Running low on food supplies, he turned to online shopping, organising a delivery for later that day.

The troubled young man never had much of an appetite, which explained his slim physique and also accounted for how he had been living so cheaply. After he had completed his shopping, Connor started to feel as though he'd taken a step backwards, reverting to reclusively confining himself to what his late friend Fred Smith described as "Cyber-Hibernation".

His frustrations increasing, Connor decided to use the internet constructively to help him try and combat his psychological conditioning. He started by simply searching "How to leave the house with anxiety".

The search engine Connor used advised him to focus on breathing exercises and assess which situations troubled him the least, and start to familiarise himself with them by repeating them. However, this advice did not help Connor. He knew he would never venture into South Town Harbour again.

The knowledge of how connected the small Sea-Side City was had polluted his mind with a fear of encountering someone from the harbour elsewhere. Each of the intimidating faces that had surrounded him was etched into his mind. Though it was less frequent than on the previous day, his darkness still loomed over him. Connor's imagination would go through bouts of seeing sinister situations where he might be recognised and targeted by the harbour dwellers.

Later that evening, on the south side of town, Shelly felt back to her old self again after successfully assisting Henry get a job. She went about her studies at the university library feeling contented, listening to music and sipping coffee as she delved into her research. Shelly had always enjoyed the scent of books; it helped her to concentrate and open her mind to take in the information provided.

After a couple of hours, she felt she had reached her full potential of study. Deciding to call it a night, she left the library. A short walk later she arrived back at the halls of residence ready to rest her blue head.

However, once she entered the corridor to her room she was greeted by a foul odour. It wasn't an uncommon occurrence for the halls of residence to have unpleasant odours. However, most of the students down her corridor had gone home. Furthermore, Shelly had never smelt anything quite as gut-wrenching as this. It smelt as though a batch of fruit had gone off. Shelly's room was at the end of the corridor, just next to a broom cupboard.

The odour seemed to be coming from the broom cupboard itself. As she approached her door, the rancid smell became unbearable. The light suddenly went out in the corridor. Shelly removed her earphones.

Suddenly the vibrating she had heard from a couple of night's prior started again, rumbling against the wooden door of the cupboard. In a moment of dreaded curiosity, Shelly nervously reached to open the door.

To her absolute horror, under the flickering automatic cupboard light, she found the grotesque sight of the caretaker for her section of the building naked, hogtied and dead, suffocated with a ball and gag;. His eyes were swollen in fear and his face covered with dried blood indicative of a broken nose.

Overwhelmed by the smell of death and the hellish spectacle of the macabre before her eyes, Shelly gasped. Stepping back in horror, she tried to run down the corridor, but was unable to escape the foul smell. Disgusted and traumatised, she tried to cry for help. Unable to get the words out, she vomited.

Eventually, she reached the front reception desk and alerted one of the night security guards who contacted the police immediately.

Within 20 minutes the police had arrived with forensics to investigate the crime scene and the obscenely displayed body of the late Sidney Walters. Once the two Criminal Investigative Department officers, DCI Peter Kent and Sgt Burt Swanson had taken Shelly's statement, she was quickly eliminated from the investigation and advised to stay with a friend for the evening.

Shelly was beside herself and more than happy to take DCI Kent's advice. However, the only person she felt comfortable enough to stay with was Connor. She felt terrible as she had yet to even apologise to him for the trauma she had put him through earlier that week. It felt slightly bizarre to Shelly, how she felt safe with him; they had only known one another for a week.

Having said that, something about the time they had spent together made her feel more connected than she had ever felt with anyone before. Too traumatised to be nervous, Shelly decided to call him to explain the situation and ask to stay the night.

Back at Connor's flat, which Shelly had yet to even visit, Connor was still awake and watching a film. He had managed to take his mind off all of his worries, secure in the comfort of his own home. Suddenly the darkened room was illuminated by the glow of his phone vibrating on his computer desk. Startled, Connor answered the phone.

To his surprise it was Shelly. He recognised straight away that something was amiss with her.

With a sniffling nose and shaking voice, she tried to explain her predicament

"Hello…Connor,

Listen I'm really sorry about the other night. It was stupid of me and I didn't understand how dangerous it was and how it would affect you. But, I, I have a favour to ask.

I've just had the worst night imaginable. There's been a murder at my halls of residence, right next to my room. I, I… just can't stay there. I've never felt this vulnerable and it sounds stupid but you're the only person I feel I can be around right now. Please can you let me stay at your place with you for a couple of nights? I never want to go back in that room again!"

After a pause of shock at the rapid change of events he had just heard, Connor reluctantly agreed to have Shelly stay round, giving her his address.

Shelly frantically packed her stuff and ordered a taxi to Connor's flat. Within 15 minutes she had arrived, but as yet unable to rid her nose of the scent of death.

As soon as she was let in, she grabbed Connor and hugged him as tightly as she could. Taken aback by the rush of emotion and unfamiliar feeling of affection, Shelly's harmless host stood frozen for a second in her arms. He didn't want to seem as though he was taking advantage of her in such times of emotional duress.

On the other hand, he also didn't want her to feel as though he didn't care for her. Connor slowly allowed himself to accept the embrace. Holding each other tenderly in a calming cradle of silence for several minutes, they didn't say a single word, their spirits tending to one another's pain, gradually allowing them to understand that they were not alone. Time stood still as their thoughts of fear and trauma started to fade, enabling them to heal in the warmth of each other's arms. Both individuals were facing their own emotional and personal challenges, and venturing into unfamiliar territory in their lives, but finding comfort in the unspoken knowledge that they would be facing it together.

S.A. BALLANTYNE

Sea-Side City

The Fragile Mask of Porcelain

The Fragile Mask of Porcelain

Cover photo sourced from:
Pexels

Originally uploaded by:
Deepain Jindal

THE FRAGILE MASK OF PORCELAIN

It was around 6 pm and young Sammy Kent was playing with his army toys in the bathroom – a tactic used by his parents to gently entice him into bath time with minimum fuss before his bedtime at 8. Innocently engrossed in his imaginative game, the 7-year old played out a fight scene from one of his favourite movies. The hero of his playset threw his evil nemesis Captain Carnivore into the warm bath water.

Tonight was a rare occasion: Sammy's father, Peter Kent, was at home. However, due to recent events, DCI Kent was unable to take his mind off work. The wholesome image of his son innocently playing with his bath toys in his safe family home was overshadowed by the horrifying sights he had seen earlier.

The previous night, the seasoned detective had gained confirmation that a twisted serial killer was at large in the Sea-Side City. This confirmation came in the form of a grisly murder. DCI Kent was among the first to arrive on the scene. The victim was a caretaker at the university halls of residence. After two decades in the force, Peter had seen his share of dead bodies and crimes. But this particular discovery was like nothing he had ever witnessed before.

The grotesque sight of the late Sidney Walters found naked and hog-tied, gagged and decaying in the confines of a broom cupboard not only took its toll on his soul as a human being, but it matched the MO of two previous murders which had occurred around the city.

None of the murder victims showed any trace of the killer's identity; the killer, though, had purposefully left traces of the other victims' intimate body fluids, smeared on the bodies and around the crime scenes.

At this particular moment in time, the killer's death toll was three. However, Peter's experience as a detective and his understanding of the pathology of serial killers led him to believe that the killer was only just beginning his or her crime spree.

Peter watched his child play. His eyes had become misty as he pondered the concept of his child playing, blissfully unaware of the horrors that the city had become home to. It wasn't known to Peter whether the killer was born in the Sea-Side City or had simply moved there. The only thing which was clear was the responsibility he and his wife shared of raising their son. They had the unenviable task of shielding him from such dangers and guiding him through life. Following his moment of reflection, Peter switched from his thoughts to his senses, and encouraged Sammy to get into the bath.

Meanwhile across town, Alex Douglas was sitting by his computer in his darkened room, his face and bare chest illuminated by the glow of his computer. He slouched back in his chair slurping a drink, with his hoodie hanging open. Awkwardly sat with one leg on the computer desk and music blasting through his headphones, he scanned through various news sources. Alex's criminology course had come to an end and he was desperately seeking other means of keeping his mind occupied.

After rescuing three people within a week, Alex finally felt a sense of self-worth. Addicted to the notion of making a difference to those in peril, he had set his sights on stopping the Sea-Side City's biggest threat. Under the influence of the high energy nu-metal blaring in his ears, Alex scoured the internet for information on the elusive serial killer. Unfortunately for would-be heroes like Alex; details regarding the killings were scarce. The police had ensured details of the murders were kept to a minimum so as not to cause additional panic to the public.

Despite the police and the press's best efforts however, fear had circulated the Sea-Side City. Fear of the unknown threat loomed in the back of people's minds. Naturally, some were more affected by it than others. But as the night sky started to darken, those affected started to feel their paranoia worsen.

Rosie Doris was just packing up for the evening, preparing herself to leave the premises of her workplace. During her life, she had worked in many different jobs; currently she was working as a receptionist at Stockbridge accountants. The 39-year old was shy and timid at the best of times. But the city's recent occurrences and inescapable reminders of the unknown threat made her even more on edge. Usually, while walking back to her grubby and cramped Jacks-Ville flat, she would be in a blissful daydream about her boss Adam Stockbridge, desperately wishing he wasn't married. Sadly, Rosie's thoughts would usually turn negatively towards herself. She was forever self-conscious about her large appearance and frizzy, unkempt hair. Tonight, however, presented Rosie with a more sinister and thought-provoking walk home. As painful as her thought process was, these days it had become even more harrowing. It felt as though the darkening sky held a heavier atmosphere. Maybe it was the collective fears of people, or perhaps it was just in her head. But she definitely felt a negative change to her emotions as she walked the streets of the Sea-Side City.

Meanwhile, in the town centre at the very heart of the city, Shelly and Connor were cuddled up tightly in one another's arms. Shelly was still shaken from the discovery of Mr Walters, the unfortunate second victim of the unknown killer, a few nights prior. The grotesque discovery had left Shelly in a vulnerable and traumatised mental state.

Being an intelligent and strong-willed young lady, Shelly

was not used to feeling this way. During her teenage years, she had shut off her feelings.

Although she considered this psychological strategy for life to be ingenious, now that she had been exposed to feelings she couldn't control or suppress, it had hit her harder than most. It felt as though the control she had gained over her emotions had been snatched from her. Despite observing countless people in vulnerable and desperate states, Shelly had never experienced it herself.

Through shutting people out and masquerading under a front of false confidence, Shelly thought she had outwitted any feelings of that nature. Subconsciously however, being exposed to emotions had become her greatest fear. A fear she was now faced with.

Luckily for Shelly, her new partner was somewhat well-versed in coping with mental anguish and trauma. Connor had suffered with severe anxiety for several years, leading a life of strict solitude. However, things were different now. He and Shelly had formed a strong and intense bond. In the short amount of time they had come to know one another, they had become connected on almost every level. The couple of weeks the newly formed couple had already spent together had been eventful and swift, as in many other blossoming relationships. But amongst the excitement and enjoyment of their adventures, there was also trouble and turmoil. In a true testament to their feelings towards one another, these times brought them closer together.

In amongst the chaos of their week and the subconscious panic that had infected the city, both Shelly and Connor had found comfort in one another's company. Connor's small but cosy flat was littered with countless films and various action figures.

Connor's geeky man cave was certainly an acquired taste; still, it provided them with much-needed sanctuary.

Meanwhile Rosie had walked to the bus stop on the north side of town. Usually she would walk the full distance in an effort to lose weight. Due to her height and weight Rosie had stood out ever since her childhood. This usually resulted in her gaining unwanted attention and hurtful comments. Alas, it was a sad reality of life. She had hoped it would get better with age; however, thus far she had experienced nothing but misery. In her trance-like state, Rosie had become distracted from the hidden danger embedded within her home city. Furthermore, she found herself temporarily disconnected from current events. At that point, Rosie realised that her bus had arrived.

"Come on love! You raised your arm, are you getting on or not?"

the driver scoffed, peering out through the open doors as the passengers left.

"Oh sorry, can I have a single to the Winston-Way Estate please,"

she asked.

Once she had paid for her ticket, she tried to recall signalling the bus as she made her way to the first available seat.

The sky began to darken as night-time crept up on the residents of the city. While many around the city were indulging their fears of encountering the depraved killer, one young man found himself relieved.

Jack Andrews had hidden himself away in the public library, enjoying the peaceful atmosphere and the unmistakable smell of old books.

He felt guilty for this feeling of relief at such horrifying events; yet he couldn't deny it was a welcome change for him. After creating a mild storm in the press after a political stunt at the university and the media's expense, Jack had become a victim of character assassination and slander from the press. In a matter of days, the confident and accomplished young man had been tarred as a racist who had instigated a small riot inside the Town Cryer pub.

The slanderous article had been published by a vengeful journalist who had been made to look foolish by

Jack's publicity stunt. This backlash would affect Jack more than most. His lifestyle revolved around the trust and compassion of a great many people. He was very much a free spirit; so free in fact, he didn't own a home or even have a registered address. Instead, he would stay with a number of different people who he had met through the years, cycling between different addresses each night. These were not just friends to Jack, they were family. Having not had any sense of family or belonging during the earlier years of his life, Jack had come to appreciate each of their presences in his life, and he did everything he could to help them whenever it was needed; in turn, he felt sure that they would support him, no matter what.

However, he was soon in for a horrible surprise. Due to the nature of the implications of the article, Jack had been perceived as a racist, a dishonest troublemaker, and an all-round political liability. Things started to escalate when camera crews and news photographers started to follow Jack around the city. The following night was a reasonably quiet night on the news front; subsequently, the whole program became an expose dedicated to finding more information on him. The news crews started to harass members of his extended family for a comment on the young upstart.

Once the people he considered to be family saw how he was being portrayed and how reporters were viewing the people he stayed with, they began to distance themselves from him. Some outright disowned him so as not to be tarred with the same brush. Others just avoided him. When it came down to it, Jack had been left with his kickboxing friends and his newly formed friendship with Ginger Taylor.

His kickboxing friends had been involved in the riot; Ginger had not.

As a new friend, Ginger had the unenviable task of pulling Jack through his time of turmoil and trying to return him to his former confident and happy self. At present, he was a hurt and abandoned child who had been betrayed by almost all of the people he had come to love.

However, not only was she there on the night of the riot, but she had spent the whole day with him and she knew that he was innocent of everything. Although their relationship was strictly platonic, Ginger felt a warmth towards Jack. In the short time that she had known him, he had managed to make her laugh and open her mind to new ways of looking at life. Sitting in the solitude of the library, the broken young man mournfully reflected his judgement as he pondered his crumbled empire of trust.

The first murder had been reported about a week before Jack made the news headlines. The victim was a wealthy old man who was found in a compromising sexual position on his luxury boat in Kingsport Harbour. Because of the man's social standing within the city and his reputation for having a rather adventurous sex life, details of his death were spared from the news reports, and the death was treated as an accident. The second victim was found at his family home under similar circumstances to the first victim.

However, the third victim, Mr Walters, had been found locked in a broom cupboard in the halls of residence, where he had worked as a caretaker.

It didn't take long for the police to establish that this was clearly a depraved act of murder. Furthermore, sperm samples of both the first and second victims had been deposited at the crime scene, thus linking the murders and serving as a signature calling card, striking fear into the hearts and minds of all those aware of the city's new threat.

Naturally, the media was in a frenzy trying to ascertain as much information as possible about the bizarre and unsavoury crimes.

At the other end of town, Peter Kent was also pondering the newspaper reports. If it wasn't for his overambitious and idiotic colleague, the press wouldn't be aware that the murders were connected. Kent's associate, Sgt Swanson, had leaked the information. Not only had he leaked the information, he'd even coined the term the Sex Doll Killer himself. Swanson was convinced that it was he who was going to apprehend the killer. Although it was clear to Kent, and a few other officers, that Swanson was behind this vanity project, he denied all knowledge. Due to the fact the journalists refused to give up their source, there was no evidence linking it to him. Nonetheless, as his wife put their son to bed, the seasoned police detective used his fear and disgust as motivation. As did Jack, he locked himself in solitude. Surrounded by books, a pile of junk food and his personal laptop, DCI Kent's improvised office allowed him to cross-reference his case notes with various forms of research.

Meanwhile, Rosie Doris had finally reached her seedy home neighbourhood of Jacks-Ville. As she walked cautiously up the street, one of the streetlamps started to flicker. The poorly lit and heavily littered street presented an intimidating environment to walk through. Hooded youths loitered on one of the street corners outside the local supermarket. Some were on bikes, others slouching aggressively, resembling primitive cavemen awaiting a physical challenge.

Although it was unlikely they were responsible for heinous crimes against humanity, they still presented an intimidating threat of danger.

Rosie felt tension building across her chest, through to her respiratory system. She felt her anxiety take over as her body reacted to the hostile environment. Hurrying towards her block of flats, she took the keys from her bag, peering around and scanning for potential danger. She jiggled with her keys, attempting to gain access to the building. The familiar Jacks Ville Union Jacks hanging from the balconies swayed in the summer night's light wind.

To Rosie, it felt as if the flags were beckoning the group's attention towards her. Finally, she managed to unlock the door and gain access to the safety of her building. Scurrying towards the lift, she tapped its button repeatedly.

At this particular moment on the south side of town, Cliff Tomlinson was sitting in front of the television. Throughout the course of the month, he had been rendered vulnerable. Usually Cliff was a very stoic, straight-talking "man's man". For decades Cliff felt he had been impervious to what he considered the emotion of weakness. He was a modern relic and to many a caricature of the ideal British male of the past.

Then, out of the blue, he had lost one of his closest friends. It had hit him in multiple ways. Not only had he lost his friend, but he had come to realise that he had taken their friendship for granted, not having seen him for several years. Understanding how precious little time he had in life. Cliff had distracted himself by turning his attention to his son's lazy lifestyle. To his surprise, his son Henry found himself a job almost immediately. This pleased him, but now his son was in work throughout the day, Cliff found himself alone in his state of mourning.

After Fred Smith's funeral and the obscene threats of death in the papers, Cliff found himself in an unenviable state of not just mourning but also dread.

He sat patiently awaiting the safe return of his son Henry. Naturally, he wanted his son to return home safe; however, it was harder to admit that he feared for his own safety. Having been a self-sufficient and capable man throughout his life, it was soul destroying to admit to himself that he was past his prime during such uncertain and tense times.

Whilst in his father's thoughts, Henry Tomlinson was too lost in his work to even contemplate the murders. Working in the Cone-ee-Island ice cream parlour, with its proprietor Shane Mahoney, Henry had found protection from the outside world. Before acquiring his new occupation, Henry, like so many other young people, had been struggling to find his purpose in life. Struggling with his weight problems and his lack of prospects, Henry had cocooned himself in the world of online gaming. He had got caught up in a vicious cycle of cynicism and hopelessness.

Much like his father, he had become something of a caricature of the stereotypical lazy youth. But through a stroke of sheer luck, Shane Mahoney had provided him with an opportunity which met his needs and improved his prospects for the future. Henry defied the stereotype he had become and exceeded his own pessimistic expectations of himself. Rising to the challenge and giving his new job his all, Henry found himself on the right track in life. With this drastic positive change in his life, he didn't have the time to even consider the obscene killer at large.

Not everyone in the parlour was as unfazed as Henry. Shane feared for the safety of his customers and his son, JJ. Due to the parlour's popularity, many of the people in the city frequented the establishment. Shane found himself becoming paranoid.

He found himself in a state of hyper-vigilance, constantly on the lookout for unusual behaviour. When he wasn't trying to identify the killer, he watched the customers enjoying themselves, something he enjoyed. Sadly, in his current state of mind, he would spend time hoping that it wouldn't be the last time he saw them. Despite the fears Shane harboured, he didn't allow his customers see this. He managed to maintain his hospitable manner. However, to compensate for his drained mental state, Shane started to spend more time out the back. In turn, Henry saw Shane's absence as a test and continued to work hard, sharpening his skills.

Back at Rosie's unsettling surroundings in Jack's Ville, she was just about to escape the confines of the lift. Her unpleasant ascent to the 3rd floor was fragranced with the stomach-wrenching stench of vomit. As the steel lift doors squealed open, the ceiling lighting outside flickered. Upon leaving the lift, Rosie felt just as anxious as she had done before entering the building. She tried to take a moment to compose herself.

Suddenly she heard the echo of the building's front door opening and the frightening incoherent voices of young men entering. Fearing that it was the youths from outside, Rosie rushed to her flat down the corridor. Her heart pounded as the adrenaline took her. She reached her flat and at last she felt the safety of home.

Locking the door behind her, she leant against the wall to catch her breath. Her chest felt heavy and her face reflected her fear, but at last she was home. Staggering into the living room of her cramped flat, Rosie all but collapsed onto her sofa. Through the window she witnessed the spectacular full moon shining brightly above the Sea-Side City's skyline.

Back at the Douglas household, Alex too was looking at the full moon. Still sitting in his darkened room, he stared into the sky.

"If there's one thing that gets lunatics going it's a full moon,"

he thought to himself.

Alex wracked his brain trying to work out where the mysterious killer may strike next.

Much like DCI Kent, Alex was trying to establish a connection between the two victims. Apart from their sex and the method of execution, the victims had nothing in common. One was an extremely wealthy retired businessman, the other a working class janitor. Though neither of the victims were young, there was a considerable age difference between them. The first victim had been found murdered on his property, whereas Mr Walters had been murdered at his place of employment.

While Alex's mind was in overdrive, he juggled with his

portable battery charger as he stared into his computer screen. Throughout the space of a couple of months, Alex had trained his body to stay active while he was deep in thought.

In doing so, he was subconsciously heightening his reflexes.

At first, he could hardly catch it at all, but now he never dropped the charger. Suddenly his phone started to vibrate. It was his new friend, a young man named Osgood. The two had become acquainted after Alex had rescued him from being knifed in the chaos and confusion of the Town Cryer riot a few weeks earlier. Osgood was new to the Sea-Side City and lived out on a small neighbouring island.

Alex had taken down Osgood's attacker and given him enough money to get home. Traumatised by the ordeal and extremely grateful for Alex's assistance, Osgood felt indebted to his hero. After contacting Alex to confirm his safe passage back home, Osgood was eager to get to know his rescuer. Not only did he feel indebted to him, but much like the island he lived on, Osgood felt almost invisible to the outside world. He had come to realise that he desperately needed friends.

He had initially contacted Alex to arrange a meeting so he could repay the taxi fare. As luck would have it, Alex was also in dire need of new friends. His only other friend was a vagrant named Charles Cartwright. Once Alex and Osgood begun talking on the phone, they realised they had similar tastes in music. After only a short while, their overseas friendship had developed over the telephone.

Alex answered the phone; his new friend was calling him to break his cycle of depression, loneliness and paranoia. Having watched the 6 o'clock news and been reminded about the bizarre killer at large, the idea that the killer may have lived on his home island had started to haunt Osgood'.

He tried to tell himself that it was ridiculous. However, as time progressed into the darker hours of the night, the fear had manifested itself, causing his anxiety to react. He had called Alex with the intention of trying to distract himself from his dark thoughts.

He made frantic attempts at small talk in order to conceal his fears. Despite his best efforts though, Alex picked up on his anxiety and turned the conversation to the unknown killer. Once Alex had breached the subject on almost everyone's mind, Osgood dropped his façade.

A strange combination of relief and vulnerability engulfed Osgood. In an instant he opened up to Alex about how the sinister threat had affected him throughout the night.

The news reports had confirmed that the murders were connected, but further information and leads were limited. Although little was known about the murders, the media were well aware that people would be hooked on the story. The people of the city were desperate for updates regarding what had happened to ease the disruption which had affected their lives. With the public demand for coverage and a lack of facts, the news broadcasts became dedicated to dwelling on the unknown.

In a desperate attempt to console himself, Osgood had scoured the internet for solutions. His search had led him to discovering a website that allowed him to view public CCTV cameras around the world. He confessed to Alex that he had been watching the cameras on his street corners for hours, looking for anything suspicious.

Alex's head started to throb with the speed with which it was processing what he had heard. The fear in Osgood's voice had made him more determined than ever to help identify and apprehend the killer. However, the revelation that Osgood had access to a website which allowed him to view CCTV cameras in the most filmed country in the world really inspired him. Alex had been patrolling the streets on foot with Charles, looking to help people in trouble. The idea that Osgood could update him on current events from afar filled him with new-found hope for his "Night-Coat Initiative".

Back at Rosie's flat, deep in the heart of Jack's-Ville, Ms Doris's heart rate had returned to its natural rhythm. In her mind, though, she was still reeling from the fears invoked on her journey home.

Slowly rising from her chair, breathing heavily, she started to sob. Despite the darkness and hostility of her local surroundings and the looming threat that hung over the city; her tears were for another reason entirely. Alas, they were tears of love, tears of hopeless love. Rosie had never experienced love before. Owing to her past experiences with people and how cruel they could be, she had shied away from it.

This all changed once she started to work for Adam Stockbridge. He was an ambitious, handsome 35-year old who had successfully built up his own financial advisory company. Adam had a full head of well kept, blonde hair and dark blue eyes and always well-dressed. Adam was the embodiment of Rosie's dream man. Unfortunately, he was married. When he had mentioned his loving wife and child, it hadn't been a surprise. She came to terms with the fact moments after he had disclosed it.

She often dreamed and fantasised about her boss, but she knew that it wasn't meant to be. Rosie liked his wife and adored seeing their new-born daughter whenever they came to the office.

The Stockbridges were the epitome of a happy family.

Being a dedicated family man, Adam was motivated to expand his business and improve their lives. Because of this expansion, he required another financial advisor in order to cover his increasing client base. Rosie was secretly hoping he would train her for the role and employ a new receptionist. Sadly, her ambitions would not be realised, Rosie didn't possess the financial knowledge, business acumen or confidence required to advise clients. Before she could even pluck up the courage to ask, Adam had employed a new candidate to fill the role: Megan Turner.

Self-assured, university-educated and with years of experience in financial work, Megan served as the perfect candidate. Mr Stockbridge's new employee was the polar opposite to Rosie in both personality and appearance.

Megan had a perfect hour-glass figure, social charm and the ability to achieve whatever she set her mind to. It was almost as if she was a cruel caricature of everything Rosie had ever wanted to be. Megan barely even acknowledged Rosie's existence. But her professional results were making Mr Stockbridge very happy.

As the months went on and their working relationship developed, Megan started to see her boss in a less than professional manner. Underlying tensions started to emerge between the two. Both Adam and Megan were leading very different lives.

Adam was starting to feel the stress and strain of his role as a father and a husband. His happy family life had turned into a barrage of bills, sleepless nights, and what felt like a loveless marriage. He felt trapped as his vitality was drained.

In stark contrast to Adam's stress-filled family life, Megan was enjoying the fruits of her labour.

Ms Turner's life was completely free from responsibilities or family commitments. Her success had brought her to a very positive place in her life. She had friends to socialise with, a luxurious purple sports car and a passion for exploring new adventures.

Despite having all the opportunities in the world at her disposal, Megan found her forbidden attraction towards Adam starting to consume her desires. The mutual attraction between them eventually led to the inevitable passionate affair. Adam had become so resentful of the pressures in his life that he didn't even consider his wife and child.

While their affair continued, Adam felt rejuvenated by

the reintroduction of passion into his life, just as the combination of passion and danger made Megan feel more alive than ever.

Sadly, after a few months, the Stockbridge family was no more. Mrs Stockbridge was left heartbroken at the revelation of her husband's affair. Worse yet, she was left almost entirely alone to cope with the added responsibilities of raising the child of the man she loved. Meanwhile, Adam and Megan continued their passionate affair.

Rosie had also become affected, witnessing how cruelly the hands of fate could turn happiness to sorrow. She felt terrible for Mrs Stockbridge. Yet she couldn't help feeling guilty. Despite how much pain Adam's soon-to-be ex-wife was going through, Rosie felt more pain for herself.

In Rosie's mind, it felt like as much of a betrayal to her as it was to Adam's estranged wife. She had idolised and adored him for what felt like an eternity. Then, all of a sudden, a complete stranger comes into the workplace and seduces him. Worst of all, after getting a taste of respect and appreciation, Rosie found herself being ignored by both her boss and his mistress.

She had grown to feel invisible.

Although she had suffered many forms of abuse growing up, she was never deprived of human acknowledgement. She felt like an outdated piece of office machinery, not even worth the effort to throw out.

Sitting in her sofa stewing deeply in her experiences, Rosie felt the sorrow coursing through her soul slowly turn to anger. Rocking back and forth, she recalled her birth name: Harriet Henderson.

She had changed her name in later life in order to move forward and leave the pain of her childhood behind. But she had finally come to terms with the fact that she never would. Over the course of her life she had developed many coping mechanisms, both as Harriet Henderson and Rosie Doris; however, pain, misery and emotional dissatisfaction had followed her throughout her life. No matter how much she tried to repackage herself, she was unable to escape her past feelings. They only got worse.

To compensate for the ever-evolving and relentless hardships life forced her to endure, she had undergone certain psychological transformations as of late. Her mind had created a new personality to bear the burdens of her life. It was a personality born out of hatred and contempt for the world which had caused her such anguish. This new mental entity had reclaimed the name Harriet Henderson. The thought of conforming to society, and cowering before life's challenges, and sacrificing her identity enraged her new alter-ego which, having reclaimed her birth name, was slowly taking control of her being.

Rising from the sofa, the mental metamorphosis was complete. Empowered with a sense of purpose and assurance which Rosie was never able to feel, Harriet was in complete control. Taking off the coat and cardigan Rosie wore to try to conceal her large appearance, Harriet began to peel back Rosie's layers of conformity. Wiping the perspiration from her forehead, she exhaled deeply, her body sensing relief. It took a moment for Rosie's body, flustered and anxious, to reflect the dominant confidence of Harriet. Now, striding purposefully down the corridor, she opened the door to her bedroom.

Upon entering, the freshly awoken giant took a moment to take in the surroundings.

At first the room appeared normal. All that was in view of the doorway was a double bed, and beige wallpaper. However, much like the fragile façade of Rosie Doris, the room took a sinister turn. As Harriet entered, her lair became more evident. There was an enormous display of china dolls populating the back wall of the room. Each exquisitely designed doll was unique. Dozens of them occupied the room, each with its individual pose. However, they were also strategically positioned out of view from the window. This made them as invisible to the outside world as Rosie's darker personality. During her troubled childhood, china dolls had held deep significance for Harriet.

On Harriet's 4th Birthday, she was given a china doll as a present. She loved and cherished her. The doll's thick brown hair, red silk dress and blue eyes enchanted her. Harriet named it Rosie after its rose-coloured dress. Due to her lack of contact with other children, Rosie was the only friend she had. As she got older, her social situation only became worsen. Eventually, she found herself envying the doll: envying how it looked, its perfect smile and slender figure. She would pretend she was the doll, and spend her pocket money to buy new dolls.

In the solitude of her home, she was creating the life she had always wanted for Rosie. It empowered her with an element of control she was unable to gain over her own life. Harriet still harboured hatred towards the doll. However, despite how she felt, she kept it at the centre of the display. Directly below the doll, at the centre of the display, on the floor, there was a large doll's house.

Harriet crouched down and turned on a switch. The walls of the house were closed, but a flickering light shone through the windows.

Suddenly, a stone ricocheted off of her bedroom window, cracking the outer layer of the double glazing. Slowly standing from her crouched position, Harriet went to investigate. It was a group of youths outside throwing stones at random windows around the Winston Way estate.

Meanwhile, in the heart of town centre at Connor's flat, Shelly was quizzing her new lover about his collection of action figures.

"You've got like 20 of these things! What do these toys mean to you?"

Shelly asked, curious as to why a man of his age had such a childish display.

Offended at her description, Connor replied:

"They're not toys, they're collectables."

Smirking at his defensive response, Shelly encouraged him:

"Alright dear, just answer the question."

Connor's face dropped, defeated in his attempt to cause an argument to divert Shelly's attention away from her initial question. He paused for a moment. The introverted young man's pale blue eyes darted around as he weighed up the potential embarrassment of answering honestly.

Shelly had become accustomed to Connor's expressions of internal conflict in the short period of time they'd been together. Placing her hand on his leg, she softly reassured him:

"I promise I won't judge you. I know I can be harsh to people in the outside world, but I really want it to be different between me and you. You're the only person I've ever been able to feel vulnerable in front of. More importantly, you're the only person I would feel safe feeling vulnerable with again. I'll understand if you don't feel ready, but I want you to know I'll never judge you for dealing with what you've been through."

Connor took a second to digest what Shelly had told him. Her words had resonated within his soul. In his brief but troubled life thus far, he had never felt so attuned to another person. Nodding his head, he embraced her, much like on their second meeting in Penelope Park.

His voice trembling, Connor explained:

"Basically, they make me feel safe and not alone. Before I met you and Fred, I never had anyone to talk to or do anything with. I had to go to work around the country at various venues doing various catering jobs. During the past few years, I've been hiding in plain sight from everyone in these jobs. People would sometimes treat me badly and then I'd come home to a bare and empty flat. See, all the years I've been crippled by my mental state; I've hidden myself to blend in out there.

When I came home, I wondered why I even bothered. Then, one day on the way back from work, I saw this film from my childhood. It was from the '90s, before all the fear and responsibilities of adulthood had taken over my life. I bought it online because I wasn't ready to leave the house outside of working hours. I enjoyed it so much I bought a model of one of the main characters."

Reflecting on his collection, Connor continued:

"After a while, I started to buy more and more models. As unbearable as the outside world was for me, I managed to turn my room into a safe haven, filled with characters and sentiments that inspired me to get through it all. Seeing as it led me to you, I'd say they've done a good job. I just wish I could thank Fred for helping me to get to you."

Shelly's striking green eyes started to tear up; fortunately she wasn't wearing her usual mascara due to her state of hibernation over the last few days.

"You're definitely not alone anymore!"

she exclaimed, wiping the tears from her eyes. Chuckling at the unfamiliar sensation of crying, she continued:

"Look at us, the perfect picture of romance."

Connor started to laugh with her as they cuddled up in their pyjamas. After a few moments of reflection, Shelly came to terms with her state of shock, similar to how Connor had come to terms with his traumatised conditioning. Suddenly she asked:

"How much time can you afford to take off work?"

Connor quickly responded:

"I can afford a few months. I've spent a lot on figures and films, but I've saved enough for rainy days that never came."

Shelly's face lit up as a new idea crossed her mind. Turning to face Connor, she eased him into the concept of her extensive recovery plan:

"I think we can grow from this, together. In the past,

when I've wanted time to recuperate or reflect, I used to travel. By the sounds of it, your reclusive lifestyle has more to do with this city than anything else. I've always found that with every new place I travel to, I find more of myself."

Nodding in agreement, Connor listened to Shelly's plan. Following Connor's late friend Fred Smith's funeral, Shelly suggested that they both take time to travel the world. Though initially terrified by the notion of embarking on such an adventure; the prospect of developing and growing with the woman he loved kindled an ambition to experience it.

They both appreciated it would take a lot of planning and research. While Shelly was willing to take a gap year from her studies; Connor realised that he would have to take a lot of time off work. Nonetheless, he was willing to risk it for her. The idea of pursuing this new goal together radiated the atmosphere. Having nurtured each other through their times of need; Shelly and Connor were able to cultivate feelings of hope and opportunity, in spite of their hostile and fearful situation.

Further north in the city, a more superficial romantic occasion was taking place.

Mr Stockbridge felt like he had been teleported back in time to his teenage years. Sprawled out on a comfortable leather sofa in Megan's lavish flat; Adam awaited in anticipation as his seductive and alluring mistress was preparing herself for a night of pleasure.

She carefully applied her make-up taking her time to build upon the suspense of their latest encounter, Megan admired herself in the mirror with each artistic stroke of mascara.

Her dyed blonde hair glowed in the light of her illuminated mirror. The darkness of her eye makeup complimented her hazel eyes as she stared longingly at her perfect appearance.

She couldn't wait to see the desire in Adam's eyes when

she finally revealed herself.

At times, Stockbridge was so besotted with Megan that his mind was almost completely void of guilt regarding his wife and child. However, the feelings of euphoria usually subsided shortly after intimate encounters with his mistress were concluded. This was one of the reasons she took so much time getting ready. She wanted to savour every moment during which she was his soul's desire. Although she had successfully seduced Adam, his guilt and remorse regarding his estranged wife and child made her feel underappreciated.

Megan's superficial need to be the sole captor of Adam's romantic desires motivated her to exceed his every sexual desire.

Despite her stunning appearance and enchanting charms, Megan had started to see everything in life as a competition. Furthermore, she was unable to understand that no matter what she did, she could never erase the years of unconditional love and trust that had been built up between Adam and his estranged wife or his natural instincts towards his daughter.

As Megan prepared herself, Stockbridge scoured through the television channels, trying to contain his testosterone-fuelled excitement at what escapades the night may bring.

Suddenly, he felt a silky blindfold impair his vision.

Across town, Alex Douglas had just been informed by Osgood that a suspicious-looking man was loitering near the Town Cryer pub.

The mysterious onlooker had been standing perfectly still for almost 10 minutes, staring intently at the premises. Osgood noticed that he hadn't once broken his gaze to look around or check the time, so it didn't seem likely that he was waiting for someone.

Upon receiving the update and checking the footage on his computer, Alex slipped into his favourite lightweight summer jacket and packed it with the appropriate improvised weapons. His trusted black tubular battery charger and a small concealable spray can of deodorant were Alex's preferred weapons of choice. Before leaving, he scanned through the usual locations his friend Charles had selected for the night. Charles stayed near payphones; he had implored Alex to keep him posted of any "Night-Coat" related outings. Alex discovered that Charles was only a few streets away from the Town Square. He hesitated for a moment.

Noticing Alex wasn't calling the payphone, Osgood asked:

"Aren't you going to ring him first?"

Alex donned his jacket hood and answered:

"If he finds out I'm going down there to take down a potential serial killer, he'll only try and stop me. From where he is, he could make it down there in five minutes. I need to do this alone. Give him a call when I get there and keep me posted if the watcher moves."

Osgood stuttered with panic, but before he could articulate his concern, Alex ended the call. He felt fearful for Alex's safety, but he was also worried he may lose his only friend if he didn't respect his wishes.

Alex opened the zip pocket on the inside of his jacket. He loaded it with his mp3 player. Then, he placed his phone in a zip pocket in the left arm.

His left earphone was plugged up to his mp3; the right earphone had a built-in microphone and was connected to his phone so he could talk to Osgood.

With his music at top volume, the hopeful hero left the house with haste. After 20 minutes of nu-metal and power walking, he reached the town square.

Osgood was still dutifully watching the mysterious stalker lurking in the town square, his shoulder length greasy black hair was soaked in anxious sweat. He waited with bated breath as Alex drew nearer to the area, reaching for his phone he started to dial the number for the payphone nearest to Charles. Not taking his eyes off Alex's screen, Osgood put the phone to his ear. To his horror, the line was engaged.

"No, no, no! Who the hell uses payphones anymore?!"

the petrified young man yelled as his hazel brown eyes darted to Charles's camera feed. What appeared to be a drunken woman had knocked the receiver off the hook.

Osgood's hands shaking with anxiety, he called Alex's mobile.

To his relief, Alex answered the call. Osgood informed him of the situation, expressing concern for his safety. Alex tried to reassure his friend, indifferent to how hazardous approaching a mysterious stalker may be. His months of training and extensive research into martial arts and improvised weapons fighting had armed Alex with the confidence to continue his investigation.

Ending the call once again, he continued his approach.

To Alex's relief, the unknown man hadn't moved an inch. Standing so still, it didn't even look like he was breathing. Alex took a moment to observe his potential opponent. He had a tanned complexion, yet his haunted expression made him look drained. It was as if the man was a lifeless shell, staring blankly into his own personal abyss.

Readying himself for whatever repercussions may follow, Alex enquired:

"Hello sir, what are you up to this evening?"

To his surprise, the ominous watcher answered, maintaining his intense stare:

"Remembering."

Alex, reflecting on the mysterious man's answer, continued his enquiry:

"Remembering?"

At that, the man wheeled to face Alex, his piercing blue eyes meeting Alex's as he exclaimed:

"Remembering the loss of Jeremy Floss! He was my son; he died right outside that pub in a riot last week. No one else remembers, but I do."

Finishing his explanation, the mysterious Mr Floss turned back to face the Town Cryer pub.

Just as Alex was trying to process what he had heard, his train of thought was derailed.

*SMASH! *AGGHHH!

The piercing sound of smashing glass followed by a shrill male scream could be heard coming from one of the dark, uninhabited back alleys veering off behind the town hall. Alex turned to investigate; no one else had heard it and Mr Floss had returned to his trance-like state, the people in the pub were oblivious and there wasn't another soul in earshot. The conditions were perfect for Alex to have his moment. Feeling a rush of adrenaline, Alex sprinted towards the source of the commotion.

Within seconds he reached the scene of the crime. Stopping to investigate the area where the glass had been shattered, Alex unzipped his left arm pocket to contact Osgood on his phone.

As his hand reached into his pocket, he was grabbed from behind and thrown to the floor. His adrenaline pumping, Alex rolled back to his feet to face his unknown attacker.

A familiar, yet displeased, voice exclaimed:

"What have I told you about going after people on your own?"

Charles emerged from the shadows, it was clear his mood was less good-humoured than usual. Alex took a moment to assess what was happening; confused and concerned, he asked:

"What are you doing here Charles?"

Anxiously awaiting Charles's response, Alex reached into his pocket for his spray can.

Charles mocked Alex:

"I've been in combat situations around the world. Do you really think deodorant is enough to take me down? I'm here because of you, son. Your mate across the sea rang me, at his wits end. You wanted to go and hunt for a serial killer and you knew damn well I wouldn't have allowed it."

Anxious at the prospect of the potential killer escaping, Alex interrupted:

"Look Charles, I heard screaming, I get you're trying to help, but we could stop…"

Charles stopped him dead:

"What you heard was a distraction that I knew would get you up here and hopefully stop you being such an inconsiderate prat!

Hunting a killer!

Who do you think you are, the Scarlett Pimpernel?!

From what's been said in the papers, this isn't a regular killer. It's a sicko!

A sicko that's creating fear across the whole county! Fear creates irrationality and irrationality creates mistakes."

Alex lowered his head in reflection at what Charles was saying. He realised how his emotions had clouded his judgement and caused him to act irrationally. Taking a moment to comprehend how he had been duped, Alex let go of his spray can. Charles lowered his voice to a more acceptable level:

"Look mate, I know you want to help people and make a positive difference. But chasing the unknown with no evidence or understanding of what you're up against is only going to get you hurt. The chances of you running into the killer are extremely slim. He's been offing people on private property. But the city's in panic. You won't be the only one looking to fight your way out of the feeling. I've seen too many brave young men become crippled or die. I don't mind admitting that I'm terrified of seeing the same for you."

Coming to his senses and realising the error of his ways, Alex nodded in agreement. He started to appreciate the quality of his "Night Coat" team. Osgood had his best interests at heart, providing him with as much information as he could. Furthermore, Charles's life experience, his rational and seasoned combat experience allowed him to monitor Alex through his questionable endeavours; ensuring that Alex was not only physically safe, but being rational.

Satisfied with his protégé's reflections, Charles composed himself and reassured Alex:

"Hey, there are plenty of people out here in this city that you can make a genuine difference by just being in the right place at the right time. If you end up hurt or killed, that's just going to hurt the people you care for. It won't help anyone! Now let's find something more productive to pursue."

With that Charles and Alex ventured off deeper into the city, under the watchful eyes of Osgood via telecommunications. While the "Night Coats" faced their collective fears patrolling the streets together, Burt Swanson was suffering the consequences of his own actions.

All alone in his humble home on the outskirts of the city, Sgt Swanson was unable to sleep.

His mind was haunting him with its own interpretation of the monstrous media entity he had created in the press. Currently, the police had very little information on the killer. Thus, the confidential information he had leaked to various media sources had been exaggerated with fiction.

Swanson was desperate to apprehend the killer and make a public name for himself. Sadly, his desperation, combined with a lack of new facts, caused him to start believing the press's exploitative portrayal of the sinister and elusive killer.

During the day and when on duty, Sgt Swanson was a highly confident, opinionated young officer of the law. But once he was away from the watchful eyes of his peers, things changed. He had no one to impress. In the darkness of night, he was left with his own insecurities and no one to distract him from them.

The concoction of insecurities and the elusive monster he was trying to capture, mixed with the subconscious guilt of leaking information to the press, caused Swanson's imagination to terrorise him.

As irrational as it was, he couldn't help but fear that the killer was aware that he had leaked the information to the press. Suffering from night terrors, he imagined a man resembling a mannequin watching him through his windows, trying to get into the house, and even killing him. Recently, the increasing bouts of mental anguish had led him to suffer from insomnia. Although the scenario differed each night, the imagery of the unsavoury stalker was the same: a masculine figure dressed in black overalls, his inhuman plastic face fixed solely on Burt, a harrowing pair of blue plastic eyes constantly watching him.

While Sgt Swanson internally tortured himself thinking of the monster he had helped create, the real killer wasn't even aware of his existence. Meanwhile across town, Swanson's more experienced partner, Peter Kent, had managed to get some sleep. DCI Kent could tell that the murders would only increase with time, and that it was prudent to get as much rest as possible before he was called out to respond to the next victim. At this point, the night sky had reached its darkest.

Back at Meg Turner's luxurious home on the north side of town, the passionate lovers had just concluded an intimate encounter.

Both Adam and Megan panted as sweat dripped down their naked bodies. Lying in the comfort of a silk-covered queen-sized bed, they shared a moment of silence. In the few short months they had been seeing one another, Megan had grown to become most anxious during these times of silence. Once the magic of their sexual encounters wore off, Adam would often go into a funk of guilt and regret.

His state of despair after such encounters made Megan feel vulnerable and inadequate. As the silence progressed, tension started to build. In contrast to the candlelit erotic atmosphere that had been created, neither party wanted to speak through fear of the repercussions of what they might say. Although they did not voice their feelings, it was clear that neither of them felt comfortable in one another's company. A frantic ringing of the doorbell broke the tense atmosphere. Keen to distract himself from his true feelings, Adam shot out of bed and put his bathrobe on.

Sniffling and wiping the guilty tears from his eyes, he said:

"I better see who that is. I don't want you going to the door when there's a killer on the loose."

Adam tied his robe and hastily left darted out of the room. Reaching to unlock the door, he hesitated. As a precaution, he armed himself with one of Megan's umbrellas in case it was the killer. Taking a deep breath, Adam opened the door.

Upon opening it, Adam exhaled with surprised relief.

It was Rosie Doris.

Confused, Adam asked:

"Rosie? What are you doing here?"

At that moment, he noticed that she had a large brown leather duffle bag.

"Please Adam, I didn't know where else to turn to. There are people loitering outside my flat. Could I stay here tonight?"

Rosie asked, with panic and desperation in her voice.

Adam took a moment to consider both Rosie's and his own situation. Even though it wasn't his property and he didn't really have a right to do so, he decided to grant Rosie's request. He thought the additional distraction may allow him to further alleviate his guilt.

Delighted at his invitation, Rosie thanked her boss profusely.

Adam scurried up the corridor to break the news to Megan. On returning to the bedroom, he found Megan sitting with a cigarette in her mouth. She had already heard what had been said and she was not happy. Her face was contorted in anger. Seething, she gave him a piercing stare.

"How dare you?! This is my flat; I don't want some fat bird leaving her sweat stains everywhere!"

she whispered sharply.

Stunned at his controlling mistress's self-centred attitude and harsh comments, Adam froze in panic. Although he had invited Rosie to stay under selfish pretences, Megan's uncaring and hurtful comments had shocked him.

After taking a moment to compose herself, she stubbed out her cigarette and added:

"She can stay tonight but I want her out by tomorrow morning. But, listen, I've been kind enough to let you stay here, don't take advantage of my charitable nature again or you'll be homeless as well."

With that, Megan got out of bed and put her dressing gown on. Opening the bedroom door, she found Rosie standing half way down the corridor. Her timid guest had probably heard everything she had said, but Megan simply didn't care. Standing in the doorway with authority, Megan curtly addressed her unwanted houseguest:

"Right, you can stay for tonight. But Adam and I will be entertaining privately and we don't want to be disturbed."

Pointing her finger across at the room opposite she continued:

"That's your room; there's an old mattress in there. It's a bit of a mess but we weren't expecting you, were we?!"

Clearly intimidated by her hostile host's abrasive attitude, Rosie slumped.

"Thank you. Sorry to impose,"

she replied, her voice breaking slightly as she carried her large duffle bag to her accommodation for the evening. The room was extremely cramped and stuffed with old furniture and tat. Sitting down on the sweat-stained mattress Rosie caught her breath for a moment. She took off her right brown leather glove. Underneath the glove she was wearing a skin-tight plastic suit.

In the privacy of Megan's unmonitored cubby hole, the fragile guise of Rosie Doris started to crack once more as Harriet Henderson started to emerge from the dark corners of her soul. Adjusting her posture and staring blankly, Harriet proceeded to unpack her large duffle bag.

While Harriet broke free from the timid masquerade of Rosie Doris, a few yards down the corridor, behind Megan's closed bedroom door, there was a tense and troubled atmosphere developing between Adam and his mistress. Watching how Megan had treated his trusted employee in her time of need had made him feel very uncomfortable. It had also caused him to see her in a different light. Furthermore, it was becoming ever more difficult to escape his guilt. Megan was feeling betrayed and embarrassed; she could sense Adam's attraction for her steadily draining away. The humiliation of being underappreciated in front of someone like Rosie overwhelmed Megan.

In response, she grunted:

"Right! I'm going to sleep!"

Turning over to her side, she turned her bedside light off and shut herself away from the situation. Adam felt awkward and insecure. He felt bad for Rosie; however, he was too intimidated to go and talk to her. He also knew that it was just a matter of time before his feelings of guilt and heartbreak would start to re-emerge. Taking all of these aspects into consideration, he decided to turn off his light and do the same.

As Megan and Adam turned restlessly, wrestling with their emotions, both were oblivious to the monstrous and predatory threat which was lurking down the corridor. As they tamed their demons and drifted off to sleep, Harriet Henderson was silently taking on her full form as the infamous sex doll killer!

Sometime later, Megan awoke. She groggily came to her senses, becoming aware of a strange scrapping and tapping coming from the corridor. She arose from her bed to investigate. Adam lay completely motionless beside her, in what appeared to be a deep slumber. Still half asleep she staggered to open her bedroom door. Looking down, she noticed a slim slither of light beneath the frame of the closed door.

"Oh! I forgot to turn the damn thing off!"

Megan muttered as she opened the door, her eyes half open. Suddenly, her vision focussed as she stumbled back in horror. She wanted to scream, but her brain was unable to react to what her shocked eyes were seeing. Before her stood a silhouetted behemoth, wearing a tattered lace hemmed dress, its wild frizzy hair exploding down to its shoulders, its skin shining in the glow of the hall light. Megan instantly recognised it to be the figure of Rosie Doris. But she also sensed it was an entirely different entity.

Slowly coming to her senses, Megan shuffled away from the horrifying figure before her as it slowly moved closer. Moving further from the doorway and into the natural light of the moon shining through the curtains, the inhuman, motionless mask of the sex doll killer became visible.

The sight of the childlike, china doll's face staring back at Megan snapped her out of her shock. It's inhuman white porcelain skin contrasted with the peach-coloured glow of its chubby cheeks and freaky, joy-filled dark green eyes staring back at hers prompted Megan to let out a scream, the adrenaline pumping through her chest as she leapt back towards the bed.

Frantically shaking Adam in an effort to wake him, Megan realised that he was completely unconscious.

She looked back at the sex doll killer. A soul-crushing shock hit Megan as the killer reached behind the door to retrieve her large bag. Harriet rummaged through her bag, as if acting out a mime, only to reveal a syringe for her victim. Further inspecting Adam's motionless body, it became clear that he had already been sedated with the contents of the syringe.

Megan's heart sank with the realisation that this was a pre-meditated and meticulously plotted execution. In a last-ditch effort, Megan pulled out her bedside drawer and threw it at the killer, trying to push her out of the way so she could escape.

Unfortunately, the attempt was thwarted and Harriet overpowered her victim, intercepting the drawer and throwing Megan to the floor with ease. Megan being rendered unconscious, the killer took out restraining ropes and two gags from her bag. She placed one on Megan and one on Adam. Having restrained her victims, Harriet was satisfied that all possibilities of escape had been eliminated. Shutting the curtains, the sex doll killer shut the bedroom door so she could conduct her latest experiment.

A few hours later, Harriet had satisfied her sensual need to consume human life. With both Adam Stockbridge and Megan Turner dead, Harriet left the room with her bag and returned to her cubby hole down the corridor. It was there she carefully changed back into the guise of Rosie Doris. By concealing her fingerprints through wearing her skin-tight PVC body suit under her clothes, Harriet had been able to ensure no trace of her presence was left at the crime scene.

It wasn't long before she managed to leave the late Megan Turner's residence without a trace, departing the scene of the crime in the dead of night.

Evading the detection of CCTV cameras through an informed route back to her home in Jack's-Ville, where most of the cameras were broken, she finally reached her flat.
Feeling satisfied with her latest conquest, Harriet admired the sun rising through her broken back window. Inhaling deeply, she savoured the moment as she opened her model doll's house and placed Adam and Megan's intimate body fluids with the other samples she had collected as trophies, and stored her fragile mask of porcelain away once more.

Keep in touch...

@BallantyneNdp

NDP
Night-Desk Publications

www.saballantyne.com

ABOUT NDP

Night-Desk Publications (NDP) aims to produce a range of unique, fictional story content, offering social commentaries and a range of different genres.

Additionally, it will offer innovative means through which readers can engage with its content.

The philosophy behind these aims is that people can often benefit from engaging with information in different ways. NDP values individuality and innovation therefore, Night Desk Publications products will offer interactive websites to enhance the reader's experience.

(Starting with the Sea-Side City universe)

Kind Regards

S.A. Ballantyne

11th January 2012

The Messenger

THE SEA-SIDE CITY OF ROCKSHORE'S PRIMARY SOURCE OF NEWS

"SOUTH TOWN HARBOUR A NO-GO!"

Once a prosperous business outlet, South Town Harbour is now a derelict no man's land. After conducting a local survey of 150 people, 94% considered South Town Harbour the most dangerous area in the Sea-Side City. There has been speculation that the condemned harbour had become home to criminal activity.

South Town Harbour has been cordoned off from public access for around three years.

We contacted the local police for comment.

South-Town Harbour featured on a map of Rockshore.

Senior officer DCI Peter Kent stated that the area was a "no-go area". He implied this was because public safety was not guaranteed due to the hazardous conditions of the site. However, when asked about criminal activity DCI Kent refused to comment.

- Hector Diamond

Stockbridge Finances
Contact Adam and his team today for a consultation

Rockshore University
Open Days 2012
Saturday the 24th of March
Saturday the 23rd of June
Secure your future at Rockshore

UP WRESTLING UNLIMITED PRO
CHECK ROCKSHORE COMMUNITY CENTRE
FOR SHOW BOOKINGS

Cutting—Craft
Hairdressing hardware
South-Side Shopping Precinct
Open
Monday to Saturday 9AM-6PM
Sunday 10AM-3PM

22nd February 2012

The Messenger

THE SEA-SIDE CITY OF ROCKSHORE'S PRIMARY SOURCE OF NEWS

STUDENTS! HELP IS AT HAND!

University can be a scary and stressful place and student life is an important transitional time for young people. There are lots of new pressures and responsibilities bestowed upon students. If you feel that life at university is taking its toll on you, or you are faced with situations you find it difficult to deal with, never fear. The important thing to remember is you are not alone.

The university offers a free counselling services to all of its students.

Rockshore University

Open Days 2012
Saturday the 24th of March
Saturday the 23rd of June
Secure your future at Rockshore

Rockshore University logo and open day information.

Raymond Adebayo is a seasoned counsellor, who has been a resident of the Sea-Side City for most of his life. He has recently joined the university counselling team. Raymond has contacted *The Messenger* to encourage any students who are struggling to come and see him. Additionally, he wants anyone who knows of a student who is suffering from the pressures of life to encourage them to come and see him.

- Ted Leslie

SEA-SIDE CITY
THE TIDES OF CHANGE COMPILATION
TIMELINE

2011

UNTOLD LEGEND

Starts October 2011

Ends: April 2012

NIGHT COAT ORIGINS:

Starts October 2011

Ends: May 2012

2012

POLITICAL LIABILITIES

Starts: May 2012

Ends: May 2012

SURVEYING THE TERRITORY

Starts: June 2012

Ends: June 2012

THE CIRCLE OF LIFE

Starts: June 2012

Ends: June 2012

THE FRAGILE MASK OF PORCELAIN

Starts: July 2012

Ends: July 2012

????

www.sea-sidecityndp.com

Want more from the SEA-SIDE CITY?

The first instalment of:

The Sands of Time Compilation

Follow the story of a young man trapped in South Town Harbour

Available now on Amazon Books!

More information at:
www.saballantyne.com

Printed in Great Britain
by Amazon